# 100 cigarettes
## and a bottle
## of vodka

# 100 cigarettes and a bottle of vodka

## a memoir

## arthur schaller

**MALCOLM LESTER BOOKS**

Canadian Cataloguing in Publication Data

Schaller, Arthur, 1928–
    100 cigarettes and a bottle of vodka : a memoir

ISBN 1-894121-00-7

1. Schaller, Arthur, 1928– - Childhood and youth.  2. Holocaust, Jewish (1939–1945)–Poland–Warsaw–Personal narratives. I. Title.

DS135.P63S32 1998      940.53'18'092      C97-932636-2

Editor: Meg Taylor
Copy editor: Alison Reid
Design: Scott Richardson
Typesetting: Jean Peters

Malcolm Lester Books
25 Isabella Street
Toronto, Ontario M4Y 1M7

Printed and bound in Canada
98 99 00 5 4 3 2 1

*100 cigarettes and a bottle of vodka*
*—the reward in German-occupied Poland*
*for turning in a Jew.*

*To the memory of my mother, Halina, my father,*
*Chaim, and my brother, Jerzyk*

# acknowledgements

—

FOR TWENTY YEARS AFTER THE WAR, I COULD NOT EVEN talk about my experiences. When I began to tell my story, I spoke in the third person, and only gradually was I able to reconcile my past with the present. During all these years, I felt a deep desire and obligation to honour the memory of my family by describing the events of my youth.

In the early sixties, I registered with Yad Vashem in Israel* and thus began the long and often painful process of committing my history to paper. The loving support of my family, and especially my wife, who urged me to write, enabled me to finish this memoir.

My wife, Sarah Hermine, has contributed immeasurably to whatever I have accomplished during the time we

* My original manuscript is catalogued with other documents at the Yad Vashem archives in file 0.33-3057; as well, Canadian copyright for that manuscript was registered in 1964.

have been together. I am immensely grateful to her steadfast belief in me. My daughters, Halina and Deborah, and my granddaughter, Evelyn Ruth, have helped me in so many ways over the years. Ferenc Szabo lent his technical expertise in both the area of computers and in music production. My heartfelt thanks to my publisher, Malcolm Lester, and my editor, Meg Taylor.

# part one

---

ACROSS THE COURTYARD FROM THE THIRD-FLOOR apartment where I was born on the morning of January 18, 1928, was a row of dusty windows belonging to the Polish Alcohol and Tobacco Monopoly warehouse. Like most of the 380,000 Jews who lived in Warsaw at the time, we were not wealthy and lived in modest circumstances. My father was part owner of a small factory where large bales of sterilized cotton were unrolled, cut, and placed in small blue packages. Each package bore a red circle with a white cross, on which, in bold, black lettering, the trademark SZALZET ran vertically and horizontally, combining the partners' names, Szaler and Zetman, using their Polish spelling. These packages of sterilized cotton were sold to drugstores.

The business was not very profitable, and my father wanted very much to sell his interest and go into lumber exports. He originally came from Galicia, a wooded part of Poland, and he was familiar with the lumber trade. My mother was a dark-haired, brown-eyed, attractive woman of strong character, the youngest in a family of six children. Her father, an Orthodox Jew with a bushy salt-and-pepper beard, was well known in the financial circles of Warsaw as Yankel-Toisher (Jankel the money-changer). The end of the First World War left him with a chest full of money not worth the paper it was printed on. His children were destined to have to make their own way in the world.

My mother, Halina Glaschmit—Haya, in Hebrew—worked her way through high school and the Warsaw Conservatory of Music, graduating as an accomplished pianist. She began her career first by tutoring and then teaching piano. During the summer months following graduation, she found employment playing piano at a resort near Warsaw. It was there that she met and fell in love with my father, Henry Schaller. Or rather, it was he who first fell in love with her, listening to her singing while she accompanied herself on the piano. In any case, they were soon married.

Henry Schaller, whose Hebrew name was Chaim, was a blue-eyed, blond-haired man with a gentle nature. As far back as my memory reaches, I resembled him, with the exception of his triple chin and huge stomach.

My parents and I lived in the small third-floor apartment on Dzielna Street until my father sold his share in the cotton factory. At that point, our fortunes improved significantly. Following my father's entry into the lumber business, we were able to move into a larger apartment—3 Mirowska Street, No. 15—which had been redecorated according to our wishes. It presented a whole new dimension of space and sight to my five-year-old eyes. The huge living room had light beige walls with a large chandelier consisting of six glass balls suspended on a network of spidery copper ornaments. There was a telephone on the wall and a short-wave radio on a mahogany table. Best of all was the balcony, from which all the sights and sounds of the courtyard below could be absorbed. There was a white-painted kitchen, accessible by its own concrete spiral staircase. The bedroom was painted blue, with patterns of silver moons, golden brown palm trees, and galaxies of stars. The front entrance to the apartment with its marble stairs led into a vestibule, from which father's little office beckoned invitingly beyond a sprawling, old-fashioned coatstand with an oval mirror in a carved frame. That was one entrance to the living room; the other was through the palmed bedroom.

A few months after entering the lumber business, my father became the head representative of the British firm Goldberger Holtzexport, which imported lumber to England from Poland. My mother still taught music, but only to her more talented pupils. She also gave concert performances and appeared on Radio Warsaw classical music programs. I remember listening to the radio: "This is Radio Warsaw's Classical Music Program. Tonight, the pianist Halina Szalerowa will perform Hungarian Dance No. 5 by Johannes Brahms."

My mother also devoted a lot of her time to helping other people. One of her three sisters, Cecil Suskind, opened a small cake shop with Mother's help. Cecil's husband, Shmuel, was a deeply religious man, but he had no trade. They had two daughters, Irene and Mirka. With the modest success of the new shop, there was now, for the first time since Cecil married Shmuel, more food in the house than they could consume in a single day. She also took it upon herself to help clothe and feed some of the apartment caretaker's seven children.

My father was frequently away on lengthy business trips, sometimes for as long as two months. He supervised forest operations involving hundreds of men and many hectares of timberland. When he returned, there was always a present for me—a toy, a book, or sweets—and the following night I would sleep alone in the palmed bedroom while my parents slept on a great ottoman in the living room. When my father was home I was happiest, not only because he was good to me, or only because he made my mother so happy. It was because, even at that young age, I genuinely loved my father and found his company exciting and compelling.

I learned to read and write at the age of five. One of my numerous cousins, a teenaged girl named Gita, stayed with us about six months before sailing for Argentina to join her sister, and taught me reading and writing every day during her stay. The discovery of the written word brought a new and strange world into my life. One of my first books was Hans Christian Andersen's collection of fairy tales about kings, princesses, giants, and gentle old wizards who gave advice filled with wisdom and kindness. People were good, kind, and noble, and they could be trusted. That was the lesson of these fables. If they failed, it was because of their errors and limitations. Evil was something unknown, far beyond this world, and one felt sorry for it, as though it were a thing that was forever lost and unhappy.

We spent the following summer in Bilgorai, a little town in Galicia, which was close to the forests being harvested. One day, I went along with Father to watch the forest operations. The trees were felled, stripped of branches, cut into logs, and rolled down into the river below. There, the logs were tied together to form rafts, and these rafts were roped, four or five in tandem, making a train. The lumber was floated right down to Gdynia, a port on the Baltic. The men controlling the trains stayed in small straw huts erected right on the leading rafts.

My mother brought two sisters from Bilgorai back with us to Warsaw to help in our home. Sally, the older sister, took care of housecleaning and laundry, while Rosie looked after me. Sally eventually left to marry a Warsaw tailor. One day shortly before she left us, she took me along when she climbed up to the apartment loft with the laundry. There, I met Bolek Grynszpan.

Bolek, who lived on the fourth floor, was my age. He had dark shiny hair, almond-shaped eyes, and protruding front teeth, so that his mouth was half open most of the time. The marvellous thing about Bolek was his lively

imagination. We became the best of friends and were insep-
arable for the next four years. Bolek's family was not well
off. His father was an aspiring Yiddish actor and made a
meagre living selling coal.

The first time I met him, that day in the loft, Bolek
showed me a model of a ship he had made, his Meccano construction set, and a small pile of yellow sand in the form of
a volcano piled on a wooden board. The crater was filled
with some oily substance that reflected all the colours of the
rainbow. Bolek told me that in a few moments, when the
evening sun appeared behind the chimney, the Holy Mary
would play heavenly music. Amazingly, just as the sky
turned red, the sound of music rose from one of the apart-
ments below, while the oily substance in the crater of the
sand volcano shimmered, and the volcano itself seemed to
have grown to enormous proportions.

The music originated in my apartment, where my
mother was doing her daily practice, but I preferred to see
it through Bolek's imagination. My own attempts to play
the piano were exasperating for my mother. She did manage to teach me such fundamentals as reading music, harmony, and fingering techniques, but I rebelled against what
I felt to be the confining bonds of set arrangements.

Religious holidays gave me an uplifting sense of excitement and joy. Sitting at the table on Passover night, I listened to my father's voice rising and falling in musical
Hebrew cadences, reciting the story of Exodus. I dipped
pieces of walnut in sweet red wine and ate them as I heard

the reassuring, rhythmic sequences of the prayers. I especially liked the prayer, *Dayainu*...(It would have been enough), recounting the miracles of Exodus.

Mother had various traditional duties throughout the Passover Seder, and so did I. My turn came to stand up and ask the Four Questions from the Haggadah. I had learned the meaning of the Hebrew text and memorized the phrases weeks before. I recited the words I understood only in translation, as I would an enchanted password formula that I believed would open the lines of communication with God. Then my father explained why this night was different from all other nights. He said that each of us ought to feel as if he or she had personally come out of slavery in Egypt. I tried to see myself as one of the redeemed children of Israel, but I couldn't quite picture myself being enslaved in the first place.

After prayers and ceremonial hand-washing, Mother brought in the traditional dinner of gefilte fish, golden chicken soup with *kneidlach* (matzoh balls), the roast chicken itself, potato pudding, and finally sweets and dessert. At the end of the Seder, we sang joyful songs and Father divided the *afikoman* matzoh as a symbolic dessert. This special matzoh, which had been "stolen" by me (with Mother's help), was reclaimed by Father for a cheerfully paid ransom.

Religion played a significant part in my young life at this time. Among the many synagogues of Warsaw, the Tlomacki Square Synagogue was the most magnificent. As a sign of our new prosperity, my father joined the affluent congregation and obtained the privilege, reflected in his yearly membership fees, of having his own seat marked by a brass plaque with his name engraved upon it. This was quite an honour. As far as I was concerned, being able to listen to the superb voice of the world-famous Cantor Mosheh Kousovitzki was the real advantage of belonging to this congregation. I took pleasure in the cantor's aria-like prayers and then joined the other boys in the courtyard when the service became too monotonous.

Cantor Kousovitzki's voice was so beautiful that gate-crashers—Polish army officers, university students, even police and symphony orchestra members—would inveigle, even bribe their way in for the unique pleasure of hearing him sing the High Holidays services. Under these circumstances, it's not hard to understand why I was drafted by my parents to act as a passbook smuggler. In brief, I slipped my parents' membership passbooks through the high iron gates to Uncle Shmuel and Aunt Cecil. That way, they, too, could enjoy the service. I considered my activity a *mitzvah*— that is, a good deed for the benefit of others. My own personal satisfaction was of course a fringe benefit.

I attended Public School No. 24, which occupied the fourth floor of a building on Ptasia Street, two blocks from my home. This building also housed three other schools, each on a separate floor. The school curriculum in Poland in the 1930's was permeated with tributes to the president and the marshal of the armed forces. Soaked in a patriotic brine, Polish history was spiced with accounts of battles won by Poles and pounded into students by means of stories and poems by Polish writers. Public School No. 24 was for Jewish children, but except for a lesson in Judaism once a week, the curriculum was identical to that of the Catholic public schools. The religion instructor was a young man who also doubled as the physical fitness teacher.

Like most apartment buildings in Warsaw at the time, the building where we lived was designed with a central courtyard. In the middle of the courtyard was either a cement enclosure shielding a patch of flowers or, when lack of space did not permit this, simply a metallic or wooden frame for airing bedding and carpets. There, women would hang out their carpets and thrash the dust out of them with bamboo beaters that looked like big, ornate fly-swatters.

My parents bought me a new Kaminski bicycle for my seventh birthday, and I learned how to ride it in the courtyard, going around in circles while my parents looked on from our second-floor balcony. A year later, I had many other interests as well. Swimming was my favourite sport, and I filled my free time with reading and music. But next to these, I enjoyed roaming around the city with Bolek.

Bolek and I measured out the city from one end to another—all on foot. It never occurred to us to spend money on streetcars, as we could observe so much more by walking. On Sundays, we liked to go to the Vistula River, passing the Saski Garden and the Tomb of the Unknown Soldier, with its eternal flames glowing in the marble urns. Sometimes, if we happened to arrive at the right time, we could observe the changing of the guard. Then we would cross a large square and enter narrow cobbled streets lined with ancient houses. This was the Old City, leading to the King's Castle. In front of the castle, set on a high obelisk, stood a statue of King Zygmunt, holding a cross in one hand and a sword in the other. After we walked a short way down the viaduct, the massive frame of the Kierbedzia Bridge came into view. Constructed with crisscrossed black steel beams, it carried heavy car and streetcar traffic in the centre, and crowds of pedestrians on both sides. We would pause halfway across and watch the loaded barges and boats moving on the majestic Vistula River below. Among them, like a precious jewel, slid a colourful pleasure boat—*Bajka*, meaning "Fairy Tale"—its decks filled with a kaleidoscope of humanity.

On our way back home, we took a different route, passing elegant hotels and fancy stores on Marszalkowska Street. We admired the shiny black limousines parked there and tried to recognize the makers, mispronouncing some of the names—such as Chevrolet and Buick—rather badly.

The arrival of my brother Jerzyk on April 28, 1937, was followed by a *bris*, or circumcision ceremony, which was performed in the living room on the eighth day after his birth. I watched with avid curiosity how the rabbi—after pronouncing prayers and touching the infant's lips with a finger dipped in wine—took a knife out of a velvet box and ceremoniously cut off the baby's foreskin. The rabbi then placed the foreskin in an ash-filled dish and bandaged the wound. Jerzyk cried a little and then went to sleep. He, of course, was unaware and heedless of a new reality that was clear to the rest of us who were celebrating while he quietly slept. He was now a Jew.

During the following two years, I completed fourth and fifth grades, which meant the end of the public school program for those who wanted to continue their education on a high-school level. For students who wished to attend a trade school, an additional sixth grade of public school was required. I was registered for high school, and looked forward to starting after the summer holidays. My long-range plans included university, where I was to study medicine. I was to study music as well so that, like my mother, I might have both a means of bringing simple joy to others and an outlet for self-expression.

My mother and I spent the summer months of 1939 in two health resorts: Truskawiec and Ciechocinek. She was taking special baths, the most expensive of which consisted of thick black mud. We walked through carefully groomed parks and drank salty waters through glass straws. To me, the only places of interest were the swimming pool and the band shell. At night, marvellous concerts were held under the stars.

Otherwise, the resorts were boring. Conversations among the rich were repetitious and hollow to my ears. When introduced to my mother's acquaintances, I was expected to act like a perfect little gentleman, bowing and smiling. At times like these, I thought of a book I once read, where time stopped and everyone was frozen in the position they last held.

When Father came to the resort on weekends, things brightened considerably. When he laughed, and that he did often, his whole body laughed—starting with the wrinkles around his eyes, spreading through his pudgy nose and full cheeks, to his mouth, filled with shiny, golden crowns. His triple chin shook along with his stomach, and he would exclaim at the height of his merriment: "A theatre!" Father was fond of good food, good music, and peaceful, friendly relations with others.

He was the elder of two sons of Shapse Schaller of Ulanow, Galicia, who was an Orthodox Jew and a local judge among his people in the village. Father's brother, Nathan, worked as a bookkeeper for a lumber company. His sister, Hancie, and Nathan lived in Ulanow with their families. It was my father who was the adventurer in the Schaller family. He had been a corporal in the Austrian army during the First World War, and would regale us with the story of how he'd somehow had the bad luck to sink a wagonload of sugar while crossing a stream with his supply wagon. Though he was severely reprimanded, it was obvious that he had been laughing as the wagon and the burlap bags of sugar went ever so slowly…down…down…down.

German was the language used in Galicia, since it was part of Austria at the time. My father obtained his university degree in that language, which he spoke better than Polish. My mother took German as a second language in her Warsaw high-school program. German and Polish were the languages used by my parents—not Yiddish—although my parents read Yiddish newspapers along with the Polish publications.

I spoke Polish, but learned to recite Hebrew prayers for my Bar Mitzvah, which would take place two years hence when I would turn thirteen. An Orthodox rabbi with kind eyes, bent posture, and a black unruly beard taught me Hebrew prayers once a week. Rabbi Gershon came to our apartment and pointed a shaky finger at the lines from the Haggadah and Siddur texts, which I would recite in a hesitant voice.

He also taught me, or rather, conveyed to me, the importance of *mitzvah*—the good deed. He quoted a rabbi who lived in Palestine during the period in which Jerusalem was occupied by the Roman armies. When asked to explain the Torah in one sentence, he said, "Do not do to others what is painful to you. The rest," Rabbi Hillel said, "is commentary." The Hebrew lessons ceased for the summer holidays, but I looked forward to seeing Rabbi Gershon in Warsaw again.

On returning from the resort at the beginning of August 1939, we found Warsaw in an excited mood. Everywhere, people were talking about impending war with Germany. The Polish government was confident. It sounded like a tough little guy with his fists up, daring the big bully to start something.

Tables were set up on street corners, where men and

women sold little yellow-and-white-checkered squares in support of the Polish air force, which consisted of about two hundred single-engine planes equipped with machine guns. I became aware of the faith most Poles placed in the Allies, England and France, who had signed a pact with Poland. I listened to a song called "Warsaw Couplets," sung at the Mirowska Square Market by an impromptu quartet of men who sold apples from two-wheeled pushcarts: "*Anglia z nami! Francja z nami! My Hitlera w dupie mamy!*" (England's with us! France is with us! We have Hitler up the ass!) they chanted to the enthusiastic applause of shoppers and passersby.

A book entitled *Poland Without Jews* appeared in the window of our local bookstore, and a different kind of graffiti defaced the stone staircase of the apartment building where I lived. Walking up two flights of grey concrete spiral stairs to our apartment, I noticed that where previously one had been informed that "Manka Loves Franek!" now crooked black lettering spelled out the warning "Warsaw and Cracow are only for Poles! And you, Bedouins—march to Palestine!"

I knew that Zionist, idealistic Jews who took the difficult step of leaving behind their life in Poland going back many generations were looked upon with pity by most Jews of some means. Poor Jews did not have the money to pay for the journey to Palestine (as Israel was then called), and anyway, most of the Jews, rich or poor, did not seriously consider leaving their homes in Poland.

At the same time, antisemitism was rampant in Poland.

Jewish men, drafted into the Polish army as all Polish male citizens were, had to get used to being addressed as Moses by any officer or private brought up to dislike Jews. The prophetic voice of Vladimir Jabotinski, a militant Zionist who urged Jews to leave for Palestine, was drowned by outcries of "Bund," which was a Jewish non-Zionist organization. "We are Poles!" the Bundists would yell, and Jabotinski was pelted with rotten eggs and tomatoes.

My father began preparing for war by stocking our storage locker in the cellar with food and other necessities: sacks of sugar, flour, potatoes, canned meat, and a whole row of dry salamis in wrinkled black casings.

One day I was playing on the balcony, where I kept some of my things in an old icebox, and through the open window overheard my parents deep in conversation. I listened closely, for they were discussing plans for us to leave for England. They were sitting together on the sofa, looking at a bundle of documents tied with string. My father was saying, "We cannot leave Poland until the business assets of Goldberger Holtzexport have been returned to England and all contracts cancelled." Showing her the documents, Father explained that if anything happened to him, the family money was safe in bank accounts in Switzerland in addition to their life insurance policies with Assecurazioni Generali in Trieste.

Street posters, plastered everywhere by government order, were meant to educate the public about the nature of various bombs and gases. The descriptions were supplemented by multicoloured illustrations of their effects on the human body.

Polish radio commentators proclaimed: "We are ready for the war! We won't even give the Germans a button!" They reassured their listeners hour after hour with a constant stream of self-praise, consisting mainly of repeated assertions, such as: How brave we are, and how brave our government is.

Then the war started. Germany invaded Poland on September 1, 1939. The Polish army on horses and bicycles put up a brave fight against German tanks and cannon, but they had been trained mainly in hand-to-hand combat and were soon crushed under the onslaught of the German war machine. The Polish government left Poland. Warsaw was surrounded and subjected to bombardment day and night. One air raid followed another. The wailing of sirens, the ominous whistle of falling bombs, and the puffs and staccatos of anti-aircraft guns became part of our daily life for a number of weeks.

Most of the time we spent in the cellar of the apartment building, which was converted into a shelter by a line of wooden benches, mattresses, and portable beds along the winding corridors and hallways. Electric light bulbs, the normal method of illumination, were replaced by flickering candles as electric lines, along with water and gas lines, were cut by the bombardment. Here, my mother, Jerzyk, and I huddled together, listening to the rumble of houses hit by bombs and the domino-like clatter of falling bricks. My father was in charge of the fire brigade and defence, and spent most of the time on the roof of our apartment building. At night the sky was lit red by burning buildings, and explosions of artillery shrapnel could be heard most of the time.

Then, suddenly, it became quiet. Warsaw had capitulated. My best friend, Bolek, and I ventured outside the apartment, and stared at our surroundings in disbelief. Buildings were cut in half. Bathtubs were hanging in mid-air. People were cutting apart dead horses, killed in the streets during bombardment. After the edible parts were hacked away, the remains of the horses were left to rot, giving off a sickening smell, which mingled with the ever-present acrid smell of burning.

A dead man was lying on old fruit crates at the market square. His eyes and mouth were open, and there was dust on his dry, yellow teeth. His shirt was half open, exposing a metal cross hanging from a chain around his neck. The yellowish grey pallor of his skin reminded me of the colour of wax Sabbath candles.

Large bomb craters scarred the pavements, exposing broken gas pipes and water mains. Many people were now homeless. They trudged through the rubble-strewn streets, bundles of possessions on their backs, wrapped in table-cloths, sheets, or blankets. Pieces of furniture that had been saved from fire were tied with ropes to the bent backs of these destitute people. Aunt Cecil, Uncle Shmuel, and their two daughters, Irene and Mirka, were among the homeless. The apartment building in which they had lived was destroyed by fire. They came to us and were welcomed to stay and share our food supply.

With the water mains smashed, water had to be carried from distant sources. At first, we carried pails of the precious liquid from the shores of the Vistula River, a distance of about five kilometres. My younger cousin, Mirka, and I became water carriers, switching the heavy buckets from one hand to the other more and more often as we neared home. After a few days, water pumps at several locations shortened the distance we had to walk. We waited our turn in long, winding queues along rubble-filled streets.

One day sometime after the surrender of the city but before the Germans arrived, I took a long, lonely walk through the smouldering city. I reached Saski Garden, my favourite public park, which I found scarred by dugouts and bomb craters. Anti-aircraft guns pointed at the skies, silently. Some of the gun crews were still there. I picked up an abandoned steel helmet and asked a tired-looking Polish soldier if I could have it. The soldier lifted his head, looked at me intensely for a moment, and nodded listless consent.

I marched home wearing the helmet proudly, my head held high. As I went, I observed the hurrying passersby out of the corner of my eye. It seemed to me that some of these worried faces relaxed for a moment as they glanced at this boy on parade. The fun, however, did not last long. When I marched into our apartment, my tense and worried parents made a big fuss about the helmet and someone disposed of it without delay.

The next morning, along with Bolek, I visited a neighbour whose balcony faced Elektoralna Street. There, from a balcony on the fourth floor, we saw our first German. He was a gendarme, dressed in a green uniform, who was guarding the Fraget Silverware Factory across the street. After our initial curiosity wore off, we amused ourselves by throwing small stones from the balcony at the gendarme's shiny helmet. He fidgeted and kept looking up, hoping to spot us, but we ducked every time before he could see us. We had fun playing this game until the owner of the apartment noticed whom our target was. We had never seen him that angry before, as he threw us out with the stern warning never to come back.

Life under the German occupation wasn't funny at all, as I soon found out. Jewish men were being taken from their homes and sent to do forced labour, clearing the streets of rubble and repairing the roads. They were held all day without food or drink and released at day's end without pay, hungry, dirty, and exhausted. While their men were away, the families worried, not knowing what had happened to them.

Epidemics raged in the crippled city. Typhus, typhoid fever, and dysentery caused by polluted water and spoiled food were common, while the decaying human and animal bodies still buried under the ruins emitted a sweetish, nauseating smell.

One day, a few weeks later, a shoemaker set up his portable workshop in the kitchen of our apartment and started to work on a pair of my father's shoes. He took off the heels and cut holes in them. Then my father handed him some shiny gold coins. The shoemaker placed the coins in the holes and nailed the heels back on.

My father was leaving Warsaw along with some other Jewish men. They had rented a truck to take them to the territory occupied by the Soviet Union following the German invasion. There, a guide waited for the group of escapees from the German New Order to take them across the no-man's land to the city of Lvov. They were departing because it was thought that since only Jewish men had been persecuted so far, the Germans would leave the women and children alone.

On a snowy February morning in 1940, I accompanied my father to the meeting place. I watched him climb into the back of a truck, and tearfully waved him good-bye.

A few days after my father's departure, I began to run a high fever. It was typhus. The hospitals were overcrowded, and Mother tried to keep me at home, but someone reported it to the authorities and an ambulance came to take me to a hospital. At the time, I was hardly aware of my surroundings. I was fighting a losing battle with some very aggressive, menacing lines that were closing in on me from all directions. I screamed and tried to push them back, but they kept on returning. I also had the weird experience of seeing myself from above while two attendants carried me out to the ambulance on a stretcher. I had a view of the scene as if suspended just below the ceiling.

Then I must have lost consciousness, because when I

awoke to reality again, I was in a hospital bed. My mother sat on the edge of my bed, crying. I found out later that after I was taken away, she tried in vain to enter the hospital to be near me. Finally, in desperation, she climbed over the wall. She was caught by an attendant, and offered him her diamond ring as a reward for taking her to me. He helped her, but refused the ring. A doctor asked her to give her blood in a direct transfusion, in a last attempt to save my life. She did, and it did save my life. Once the crisis had passed, I improved steadily, and after a few weeks I was transferred to Leszno quarantine hospital for observation.

Shortly before my discharge about a month later, a fire broke out in the disinfection chamber located in the basement of Leszno Hospital. The women, whose clothes were being disinfected, were in the showers nearby. When the smoke started to pour from the smouldering garments, an alarm was set off, and about forty screaming women, young and old, started running up the main staircase just as they were—that is, completely naked. The women's quarters were on the top floor of the three-storey building. When I heard the alarm, I left my room. As I reached the staircase, I was confronted with the spectacle of forty naked women running by. There was swinging flesh and hair in more abundance than I'd ever seen before in my life. I was too young to have an interest in women, except simply as human beings, but this scene was to be forever embedded in my mind. What's more, the first girl confronting me laughed while running by, which offended my sense of modesty.

Homecoming at last. Mother came to pick me up. She seemed to have changed a little, in a way that was hard to define. She was more serious perhaps, and her face was thinner. To take us home, Mother hired a rickshaw, a three-wheeled cycle with a bench in the front and the driver pedalling behind.

I had seen rickshaws before, from the hospital's front window, but had never ridden in one. The day was misty. Mother sat beside me, holding my hand and asking this and telling me that, while behind us the man strained at the pedals, his seat squeaking in time with his movements. At home, I was given a warm reception by my uncle, aunt, two cousins, and my brother, Jerzyk. I was surprised how the little fellow had grown and how smart he had become. Why, he talked almost like a grownup!

There were other changes I noticed immediately upon entering the apartment. Scarceness of space was one of them. A family of German Jews relocated to Poland occupied the living room and father's office, while the kitchen served as a bedroom for Aunt Cecil's family.

The bedroom, crowded with things moved from other rooms—including the piano—was used as a bedroom for Mother, Jerzyk, and me at night. During the day, it served as an all-round activity room for everyone. Food was also very scarce. A fifty-fifty hamburger (half meat, half bread) was a treat, and bread itself was rationed. It was unbelievable that such radical changes had taken place during my three-month absence.

The day after I returned home from the hospital, the spring weather lured me outside. I took down my bicycle and rode slowly along streets close to home. The rubble had been cleared, bomb craters filled, and services restored, but the acrid smell remained, and the blind eyes of windows in burned-out shells of buildings stared in silent accusation. On my way home, a boy my age waved me over and asked for a ride on my bicycle, offering to pay 10 groszys for three circles around the market square. I agreed, and soon there was a small crowd of kids wanting a ride and willing to pay for it. Each had to wait his turn in line. At day's end I counted my profits. I had 1 zloty and 80 groszys (1 zloty = 100 groszys). I was in business for myself. It felt good.

When Jewish schools were closed on German orders, Jewish teachers organized small groups of students and taught privately in their own homes. They did this at the risk of losing their lives, if they were caught by the Germans or Polish police. My mother had found a teacher for me, and I was going through the high-school program three hours a day, six days a week. We had to use every possible avenue of self-preservation—this was perfectly clear. The Germans were obviously intent on suppressing, persecuting, perhaps even eradicating us, the Jews, both physically and culturally.

There was a startling contradiction in the way older Jews, who were adults in the First World War, still perceived a typical German as Good Uncle Fritz *mit de Sauerkraut un de Knackwurst*. They remembered helping provide German soldiers with civilian clothes, and saving them from death

as the war ended. They were shocked when a German bru-
tally pushed them into forced labour—in the streets of rubble—and treated them much worse than they treated the
Poles. These were not "their" Germans. They did not act
like "their" Germans. They did not even act like human
beings, even if their language resembled Yiddish.

On the morning of October 12, 1940, an event crucial to
the life of every Polish Jew took place. The Germans enclosed
a part of the predominantly Jewish section of Warsaw with
sharp razor wire, and posted *Schupos* at every outlet and intersection. Posters were glued to walls proclaiming that:

> All the citizens of Generalgouvernement [as this
> part of Poland was now called by the Germans]
> residing in the enclosed section of the city of
> Warsaw [called the Jewish Housing District from
> now on], who are not Jews, and have no traces of
> any Jewish ancestry for three generations, must
> move out and find quarters in the Aryan section
> [that is, the part of Warsaw outside the Jewish
> Housing District], before November 15, 1940.
> On the other hand, those persons with Jewish
> ancestry up to three generations back must live
> and stay in the Jewish Housing District at all
> times, or be shot if found outside of it.

It wasn't long until the Germans replaced the wire with
a thick, three-metre-high wall made of old bricks taken

from the ruins. They spiked the top of the wall with multicoloured chunks of glass from broken bottles and windowpanes, set thickly in a layer of grey concrete. We never
used the German name Jewish Housing District. To us, it
was the Ghetto.

The Jewish ration cards allowed 75 decagrams of bread
per person per week. This, plus some pickled red beets, was
the only legal food supply set by the Germans, and it was
far below the minimum necessary for staying alive. As food
became more and more scarce, the prices doubled and
tripled overnight. All other food had to be smuggled in
from the Aryan side. Cooked blood was smuggled in from
Polish slaughterhouses and sold, hot and salted, by "blood
vendors" on Gesia Street. Each fist-sized portion contained
life-sustaining protein.

I decided to become a smuggler. While things were still
"unsettled," owing to the movement of people in and out of
the Ghetto, I took advantage of the fact that my facial features did not correspond to the Nazi notion of what a
Jewish face should look like. Using my old school pass,
which I showed at Ghetto intersections, I left and re-entered
the Ghetto many times. I would bring back a knapsack full
of candies and other confectioneries, purchased in stores on
the Aryan side. I had to make my purchases in ten-decagram
portions, the maximum allowed to a customer at one time.
I overcame this problem by walking from store to store until
my knapsack was full. For starting capital, I used money
earned from my bicycle rental business, which continued

whenever I had time to go out to the Mirowska market square. Incidentally, the square was now divided by a wall: one half was within the Ghetto, and the other on the Aryan side. But the price remained the same, because of devaluation. It was now three half circles for 10 groszys.

Part of my profits went to my mother, who smiled at my enterprises but saw to it that I did not neglect my studies. She wasn't idle either. While Aunt Cecil and her daughters took care of three-year-old Jerzyk and did the housekeeping, she gave concert performances for CENTOS, an organization dedicated to helping orphaned children. Kitchens were set up to supplement the starvation diet. My mother also acted as a sales agent for any merchandise obtained from among her wide circle of friends and acquaintances. Some of the merchandise consisted of shoes and clothing, which had been hidden in cellars. Other commodities such as eggs and lard had been smuggled in more recently. I became accustomed to seeing bags of ladies' shoes in our bedroom one day and boxes of Passover matzohs the next.

But no matter what kind of merchandise it was, the results were the same. While rapidly increasing numbers of people, especially children, were dying of starvation, my mother managed to keep her own and her sister's family alive. Occasionally, there were letters from my father in Lvov, which was under Russian occupation. The Jews there were not discriminated against, at least not officially. He was well, and was not starving. I looked forward to his letters, which arrived with a large black postage stamp picturing a man holding a burning torch with a red star over his head.

Then, on June 22, 1941, the Germans attacked their former ally, the Soviet Union, and the letters from my father ceased altogether. Things became progressively worse in the Warsaw Ghetto. People were dying in the streets, on the very sidewalks in ever—increasing numbers, their bodies ravaged by the effects of scurvy. Some people became like skeletons covered by parchment-like skin broken by malnutrition sores. Other people suffered with bodies swollen by excessive intake of water, which they drank in a futile attempt to ease the constant, agonizing hunger. Their inflamed skin burst open, and their arms and the calves of their legs were covered with malnutrition sores.

Following a tip from Aunt Dwora's eldest son, who was a professional grinder, my mother helped me to secure a job in a factory, where I was set to work grinding and polishing parts of electrical equipment to be plated with nickel and chrome. The factory produced immersible heaters and was located in the basement of 31 Elektoralna Street. Mrs. Kanarek, the owner, had obtained a special permit from the German authorities which allowed her to operate this "essential products" factory in the Ghetto, while she herself, not being Jewish, lived outside the Ghetto walls.

I liked the job, and I liked my co-worker, whose name was David Waisbrot. He was in his early twenties and had a dark complexion, and he sang beautiful Yiddish songs as he worked. His voice mingled with the roar of the motors and the slapping of the leather conveyor belts.

Every day I earned the equivalent of a one-kilo loaf of black bread, which helped to keep starvation away within our household. Between work and study, I had little time for relaxation, but I tried to maintain a hopeful state of mind most of the time.

One day, a German gendarme fired a bullet from the Aryan side through a small opening at the base of the Ghetto wall. The hole had been left there when the wall was built so that gutter water from the Aryan side could flow into the sewer on the Ghetto side. The bullet hit the right foot of my Uncle Shmuel, who happened to be passing by. He was carried upstairs by men who saw him fall and laid on the iron bed in our kitchen, where he and Aunt Cecil used to sleep. He smiled at his wife and pressed her hand, without saying anything. His emaciated body could not stand the loss of blood, and he died two days later.

Uncle Shmuel was a gentle giant of a man, with a pronounced nose and a narrow chin sparsely covered by a goatee. Deeply religious, he had prayed every morning and observed the Sabbath and religious holidays with a firm but quiet conviction and a belief in a better world to come.

One particular incident should illustrate what kind of man Uncle Shmuel was. For a certain Jewish holiday, Uncle Shmuel acquired an egg, which would be eaten as a symbol of life. After boiling the egg, he meticulously peeled it, and divided it into seven equal parts. He then gave a portion to each member of the family.

His passing caused only a small interruption in the daily lives of the survivors. The struggle for survival did not allow for long mournings. The living competed for attention with the dead, and their needs were more urgent. Some of the poor in the streets devised ingenious ways of obtaining some sustenance. One in particular, who was widely known as Mondry Wariat in Polish, which loosely translates as Clever Madman, walked from house to house, singing: "He doesn't want to give up his ration card...*yet*! He wants to *live a little*...and *not* give up his ration card." People liked his act, and some gave him bits of food so that he could fulfil his wish and live a little longer. I thought to myself: He is successful because people identify his wish with their own.

Another man, working in partnership with a girl he introduced as his sister, walked from one apartment courtyard to the next reciting the psalms of King Solomon and King David in Hebrew. He had a marked preference for Psalm 22. "My God, my God, why hast thou forsaken me?" he would intone with feeling, while embellishing his recitation with dramatic gestures. His "sister," her hands modestly crossed, her head piously bowed, stood by reverently until the offerings of small chunks of bread, cabbage leaves, coins, and other bits and pieces began to fall from windows and balconies. The pair quickly picked up the newspaper-wrapped gifts with as much gentle restraint as they could muster. The captive audience of hungry people grasped the truth of Psalm 22 in the Warsaw Ghetto, and they responded generously. To reinforce the good impression they had just made and to solicit more gifts, the pair, their hands raised, informed their audience that they had on that very day taken a bath and were completely deloused, hence clean—a commendable act in the lice-infested Warsaw Ghetto.

Other desperate but determined people who lacked any outstanding talent but had a strong will to survive and a good pair of running legs took their chances as *hapers* (grabbers). They waited in the street until they spotted a woman carrying a loaf of bread. Then they snatched the bread out of the unfortunate woman's hands and took off, gulping the bread down as they ran. If caught, they usually attempted to stuff the remainder of the bread into the fly of their pants, hoping to discourage the pursuers from reclaiming it. The bread, incidentally, was at least fifty percent corn flour, potato peels, and sawdust.

The area of the Ghetto, which now held about 500,000 people, was just over 400 hectares. There were no parks in the Ghetto. People were crowded up to twenty per room. In the Aryan parts of Warsaw, the density was seventy people per hectare, whereas in the Warsaw Ghetto the density per hectare averaged 1,100 people!

The affairs of the Warsaw Ghetto were run directly by the Jewish Council, known as the Gemeinde, under the leadership of Chairman Adam Czerniakow. The Ghetto had its own police, services, and bureaucratic machinery. It was thus a state within a state within a state. Instructions in how to run the Ghetto were set by the Germans.

Hunger and misery and death affected me only to the extent that I had to adapt myself to meet them. Within the depths of my mind, little had changed. I still believed, as before, in the ultimate goodness of the human race. Evil hadn't stopped being something one felt sorry for, because people who were evil didn't know any better. True, the suffering of the victim was more profound than that of the oppressor, but what did the oppressor do to himself by doing these things? Can one have a peace of mind while hating? Can one have trust in oneself when distrusting humanity? Can one live with oneself while inflicting death on others?

I never doubted that the answers to these questions were all in the negative. Absolute good is here all the time, and lucky are the ones who can see it and rise above their misery. It could not be said that I consciously thought about these things. I just knew this deep inside, and knowing it was as normal to me as breathing.

The Germans decided to reduce the size of the Ghetto even further by excluding a number of streets, adding them to the Aryan part of the city. The street we lived on, Mirowska Street, already halved by a wall, was totally cut off from the Ghetto. I lost my job as well, since the factory on Elektoralna was now outside the Ghetto walls.

We were given three days' notice to move. My mother arranged for the three of us to move in with one of her sisters, Lea, and her three children, who lived in a three-room second-floor apartment at 31 Gesia Street, across from the infamous Pawiak Prison.

Aunt Lea's husband had died shortly after the beginning of the war, and she was left with his small silverware factory. The factory, now inactive, consisted of a large room filled with polishing equipment and gold and silver plating vats. It adjoined the apartment, which comprised two rooms and a kitchen.

Aunt Lea's older son, Leyzer, had been born with a mental disability. He lay in bed, his head clean-shaven, his eyes staring blankly into space. For the thirty years of his life, he had been completely dependent on his mother to take care of all his needs.

Her daughter was twenty-eight, bitter because her engagement, which had been arranged by a matchmaker with an out-of-town suitor, fell through after her father's death. Her long, thin face wore the permanently scornful expression of a person who has been cheated of her only dream.

Aunt Lea's other son was a boy of twelve who was small and quick and spent all his time, except that needed for meals and sleep, running around with some kind of a gang. Aunt Lea herself was a tired, prematurely old woman, usually dressed in a dark, worn housecoat with a wide turned-up collar. The children had come to look down on her in the years following their father's death.

My mother, Jerzyk, and I moved into this situation. Aunt Cecil, with her two girls, was now left without her stronger sister's protection. This was a crossroads for the two families. There simply wasn't enough room in Aunt Lea's apartment, and we had to separate.

My bed was in the same room as Leyzer's, along the opposite wall. One day, a month or so after we moved into the apartment, he spoke to me for the first time.

"Arthur," he said haltingly, "could you get me a glass of water?"

"Of course, certainly," I replied, hurrying to the kitchen, where I filled a glass of water from the sink. When I gave it to him, he brought the glass to his lips with shaking hands and drank thirstily until it was empty.

"More?"

"Thank you, no."

I picked up the empty glass. Leyzer rolled onto his side, facing the wall, and seemed to go to sleep. He died the following night.

Aunt Lea made small whimpering sounds as she washed Leyzer's body for the last time. The heavy dining-room table had been dragged into our room and Leyzer's body placed upon it. Rigor mortis had set in, and his arms and legs were locked in unbendable positions. So bizarre were the involuntary movements of the legs and flapping of the arms that his younger brother and sister could not restrain themselves from bursting into nervous laughter. Finally Aunt Lea joined in their hysteria, perhaps partially relieved that half a lifetime had been removed from her shoulders.

They carried Leyzer's body down to the street and laid it on the sidewalk against the wall of the apartment building, covering him with a couple sheets of newspaper. Otherwise, they left no identification. That way, the Gemeinde could not charge the family for removal and burial. Every day two-wheeled carts went through the Ghetto to gather the corpses, which were then buried in mass graves.

Rain drizzled endlessly onto the cracked pavement of Pawia Street. The usually crowded street was empty, as if swept by a giant broom. In a way, that was the reason for the absence of people at this money-changing centre of the Warsaw Ghetto in early 1941.

Let me explain. During daylight hours, one would normally see small groups of people huddled in circles or pairs—men, dressed in black and shades of grey, hunched towards each other. Occasionally, a hand would reach into an inner coat pocket, nervously extracting a bundle of paper money notes—predominantly Polish, but quite frequently British pounds, American dollars, and Third Reich German marks. All the currencies of the world found their way to the Pawia Street money exchange. Now, why was the street empty?

Armoured cars bringing new prisoners into the Pawiak Prison had just passed close by on Karmelicka Street. German drivers and Gestapo men amused themselves by banging hammers on metal gasoline cans inside the armoured car. It sounded like gunfire, and sometimes it was, leaving dead and wounded people on sidewalks and pavements. The gun-like sounds of the gasoline cans being hit by the grinning Germans caused more heart failures among frightened passersby than the real guns.

But what is the difference? Death is death. Pranks like that were perpetrated daily on the starving population of the Warsaw Ghetto—adding corpses to those already stretched out at the base of walls and covered with old newspapers. The dead were mostly children, victims of starvation, malnutrition, and cold.

Despite the desperate situation closing in on us, I somehow managed to pursue my interests in the new location. The two-year high-school program was completed in one year. With no other tutor available, and my job lost because the factory was now outside the Ghetto, I discovered a library nearby and read books at a rate of two or three in a day. My mother jokingly said that I swallowed them. The *Introduction to Psychoanalysis* by Sigmund Freud was tough stuff, but I got it under my belt along with other volumes written for much older readers.

One day a boy I met at the library took me to a building at 11 Gesia Street where, on the second floor, young boys and girls sang in a choir directed by Mr. Faiwuszyc, a fine musician. But music was not the only feature of the choir. It served as well as a cover for an underground movement, a Zionist organization called Hashomer Hatzair. I jumped in like a fish into fresh water and joined both the choir and the movement.

The Faiwuszyc Choir occupied the second floor of 11 Gesia Street, near the corner of Zamenhofa Street. The large room had an upright piano in the centre and wooden benches on three sides of it.

During my first visit there, in the late fall of 1941, Mr. Faiwuszyc asked me to sing a song of my own choosing so that he could assess and classify my voice. I chose one my mother's favourites, called "Violeta." I was a bit nervous, and sensed some tolerant smiles from the audience when I hit the high notes. Mr. Faiwuszyc soon made me feel at ease with his encouraging attitude.

I was classified as a soprano, and sang second-soprano parts in the choir, learning Hebrew and Yiddish songs at the same time. In the movement, I was introduced to the history of Zionism, the theory of socialism, and life on a kibbutz in Palestine, or Eretz Israel (Land of Israel).

One day, I was leaving the building with a few of the girls in the choir. One of them, a quiet, unassuming girl, stumbled on the icy walk and fell into a pile of snow. Some of the other girls laughed at her. I helped her up, and after that, whenever I was at a choir practice, she was always close by, being quietly helpful whenever possible.

A young woman named Hannah instructed us about life in a kibbutz in Eretz Israel. She was an idealist whose face lit up when she spoke about the beauty and historical importance of having one's own country. It was worth living and fighting for, she stated at the conclusion of each lesson.

Hannah was rather squat, and the most striking thing about her appearance was her blue eyes, framed by an unusually thick braid of blond hair, which tapered into a single ponytail. I was told by Mordecai Anielewicz, a member of the Hashomer Hatzair group, that Hannah belonged to the agricultural training kibbutz in Otwock, a farm located in the suburbs of Warsaw. She maintained contact with the Otwock Kibbutz, also known as Hahsharah. Then one day in early February of 1942, Hannah failed to show up for our Hebrew lesson and choir rehearsal. I looked forward to the lessons, and besides, I had completed a four-page biography of Louis Pasteur as a homework assignment.

As I read the closing sentence of the biography to the choir assembly, "And so, whenever we speak of people who in some measure contribute to the betterment of mankind, let us remember Louis Pasteur, who devoted his life working for the benefit of mankind," I looked in vain for Hannah.

Mordecai Anielewicz was talking to Mr. Faiwuszyc, our choirmaster. Mordka was one of the older members, meaning twenty to twenty-five years old. I approached him, asking if he knew where Hannah was. Mordka's sad face and his silence spoke more than words could express. I never saw Hannah again. Later, I heard she'd been caught by the Germans while travelling from Otwock, running messages.

The instructor, Itzak Zuckerman, tried to explain the principles of socialism to us, saying: "Look, my hat is also your hat—and your book is also my book." That I could never understand. To me, lawful possession was nine-tenths of the law, and it seemed to me that with that kind of sharing, everyone had nothing.

We were visited by a great Jewish poet, Itzak Katznelson. He told us about an enormous tree that grew near Tel Aviv. The tree was so thick that it took five people joining hands to embrace its trunk. There were only four people there at the time, including him. A small boy walked by: "Boy! Oh, boy!" shouted Katznelson. "You have long hands! Come here!" The boy blushed and ran away. "You see," explained the poet, "to be told that one has long hands in Yiddish is equivalent to being called a thief!" Itzak Katznelson had brought a unique moment into our lives that afternoon. There weren't any trees in the Warsaw Ghetto. He planted one in our minds in that terrifyingly cold, painfully starved Warsaw Ghetto in the first months of 1942.

About this time, the German armies got the first taste of their own medicine in the frozen fields of Russia. The news, secretly brought into the Ghetto, was confirmed by the next German order: "All persons possessing furs of any kind must deliver them to the German-appointed collection centres. Any person found in possession of furs after a given date will be shot."

This was good news. It was the first indication that the Germans were losing the war. I packed my mother's Persian lamb coat and her silver fox boa, both of which were bought with her earnings as a concert pianist and piano teacher, and carried them down to the basement. I buried them under the cellar's dirt floor.

Every Jew in the Ghetto had to wear a white band with a blue Star of David on his or her right arm. One could buy them from street vendors in a wide variety of designs, materials, and prices. The most expensive ones were waterproof.

The Warsaw Ghetto had an intense cultural life in spite of the oppression. There was a theatre on Leszno Street near Solna Street that was producing Lehár's operettas and plays for children. Clandestine libraries and even an eighty-piece symphony orchestra were carrying on their work. In the midst of physical human deterioration, the bodies were weak, but the spirits remained strong. There was wit, humour, and song. Many apartment tenants staged parties, using local talent to provide the entertainment. The proceeds invariably went to support the soup kitchens. Jokes were told daily about Hitler, and about the Nazis in general. One example:

A child who steals? Answer: mania
An adult who steals? Answer: kleptomania
A nation that steals? Answer: Germania!

On my fourteenth birthday, January 18, 1942, Mother prepared a surprise for us. She took Jerzyk and me to a tiny café. We were each treated to a meat patty on half a bun. Actually, she secretly brought the food with her into the café, and only ordered two cups of "ersatz tea" (burned sugar tea). The reason that we went to a café to have our birthday party was so as not to flaunt the food in front of Aunt Lea and her children.

Speaking of luxuries, there was one treat sold by street vendors for a high price. It was called Rollo and consisted of a roll of candies with caramel centre fillings within a

chocolate coating. Of course, with our daily allowance of
only about 180 calories per person, any supplement like this
would help to prolong life.

The soup kitchens, which my mother helped to support
with her piano concerts for ZTOS (Jewish Mutual Aid
Society), were also frequently providing a bowl of cabbage
soup for each of us. Sweetish, frozen potatoes and pickled red
beets were sometimes issued through the daily ration cards.

The leader of the Jewish Council, Adam Czerniakow
was, publicly and privately, an object of scorn mixed with
envy. Both of these emotions found expression in songs
such as this one:

Comrade Czerniakow has a huge belly.
For lunch, he eats chicken-noodle soup!
Every day, he travels to the Gemeinde building.
May an evil fate befall him! Ta-di-ra-sa bum!

As the one who carried out German orders, along with his
committee of twenty-four members and the Jewish police,
Czerniakow was naturally the central target of resentment.

A curious example of self-destructiveness manifested
itself in the short-lived Anti-Black Market and Anti-
Racketeering Bureau. Its members wore green bands on
their hats instead of the blue bands worn by the regular
Jewish police. The bureau was created to disrupt the source
of ninety percent of the food provisions brought into the
Ghetto, namely, smuggling operations, large and small.

Earlier, when we still lived in our own apartment at 3 Mirowska Street, one of these "Green Bandits" rented the little room that had been my father's office. He showed his true colours within a few days by verbally attacking my mother. "When I am through with you," he shouted, "you will walk on your eyelashes!"

I was shocked. But I was also fascinated by the very idea of someone walking on his eyelashes! I need not have wondered long. My mother had connections. The blustering offender was out of our apartment and out of a job the very same day! And somehow, I don't know by what means, the "Green Bandits" were wiped out of existence without a trace.

Later that year, the Faiwuszyc Choir, of which I was still a member, performed in front of a live audience. We gave a concert at Gardner's Restaurant, at Leszno, near the Tlomacki Synagogue. Adam Czerniakow and members of his committee were among the audience in the front rows, along with officials from the top ranks of the Jewish police, some representatives of ZTOS and Yiddish culture proponents. We sang a medley of Yiddish and Hebrew songs to an enthusiastic round of applause. We were each given one or two dry, brown, sugar-coated cookies in the shape of little hearts. After the concert, which took place in the afternoon, I went to the library on Zamenhofa Street along with another member of the choir. On our way, we witnessed a little skirmish.

"What a whore!" exclaimed a teenage boy as he passed a red-headed, stout woman, painted with layers of makeup and bright lipstick. She had a couple of black beauty spots on her cheek. Her eyes were lined with a pitch substance. He was obviously mocking her.

Her reaction was immediate, and the string of profanity that followed made me and my friend blush. She closed with "Wait till I get my boyfriend after you!"

The offender did not wait for the "boyfriend." He put up his coat collar and made a quick retreat. We continued on our way to the library, quietly puzzled that there still was demand or need for such services in the Ghetto.

My mother, in partnership with one of my cousins, Aunt Dwora's oldest son, turned Aunt Lea's dormant silverware factory into a grain mill. Grains of all kinds were smuggled into the Ghetto in burlap bags thrown over various sections of the Ghetto wall. It was easier to handle grain than flour, and turning grain into various products was very profitable.

In spite of the noise and dust problems, the mill was a success. Men walked up and down the stairs, bent over under the weight of their precious cargo, and we ate cereals for the first time in two years. There was a price to be paid, and paid, and paid: "drink money" going to a countless parade of Jewish policemen, who could not miss hearing the grinding noise—or the opportunity of adding to their income.

Finally, the cost of the operation, and the real danger of being discovered by the Germans—we were right across from the Pawiak Prison, the main interrogation centre for

the city of Warsaw—made it impossible for us to continue.
The mill was taken apart by the cousin who had run it. We
tried to look for other sources of income, but without immediate success. It stung my heart to discover that my mother
had had a gold crown removed from her tooth. She sold it
to buy food for my brother and me.

We recalled funny incidents from the recent past to
keep up our spirits. One of them dealt with a popular actor-
comedian of the Polish stage and screen who was Jewish.
His name was Michael Znicz, which lent itself to a pun. In
Polish, to say "*z niczem*" means "with nothing." When
Mother rented a room to Mr. Znicz, whose name sounded
almost exactly like this Polish phrase, she quipped: "I went
out with nothing and came back with nothing."

There was a new class of people who prospered in the
Warsaw Ghetto. Brush-makers were among the "newly
rich." I was invited by a boy in our choir along with other
boys and girls to visit his father's brush workshop. This was
a cottage industry within their living quarters. We were
given the opportunity to learn how to make brushes,
pulling strong twine through holes drilled in wooden forms
and tightening doubled-up bunches of pig bristles into a
functional whole. The predominant impression I picked up
in this German-sponsored factory was that of blissful self-
gratification. There was applesauce for the host's son, and
none for the guests. The skin tone of the host, his wife,
and his son was pink, not grey like their guests. The brush-
maker and his family behaved, it seemed to me, like

caricatures or parodies of pre-war Jewish members of the privileged upper class.

Mother took me along to an evening of cultural entertainment on Nowolipki Street. She played a few classical piano pieces, mostly Chopin and Liszt. I was asked to tell a joke or a story to this young group of men and women. Although I was nervous and shy, I somehow managed to recount a story of a professor who went out fishing in a boat with a fisherman-guide. The professor, true to his profession, inquired of his guide's academic background:

"My good man," he grandly asked, "do you know how to write?"

"Nope," came the short answer from the hard-rowing guide.

"Well, my good man," declared the professor, "you are missing one *quarter* of your life. Perchance," the pedagogue tried again, "you know how to read?"

"Nope," replied the guide instantly, rowing harder.

"You are missing, I dare say, one *half* of your life. What a pity," sighed the educated man. The sky was getting grey, the wind stronger. A storm was brewing and gaining strength. The small boat was bobbing up and down like a peanut shell.

"Professor," the guide interjected, "do you know how to swim? No? Well, then, you're likely to lose *all* of your life."

My little tale was, despite my jerky delivery, well received. I think that my mother was proud of me. I was certainly proud of her.

People brought into the Ghetto from other cities and small towns were lodged in communal locations where hunger, cold, and sickness were worsened by crowding and unsanitary conditions beyond belief. People in those "points" (*punkty*), as they were called, died without hope as soon as they lost their mobility. Beggars in the streets were starving and dying, but even they were better off than the thousands of men, women, and children languishing in those "points." "Pinkert's wagons" picked up the bodies lying on the sidewalks every day. The black two-wheeler and three-wheeler rickshaws became a common sight. But life persisted. Every second, every minute of life snatched from the finality of death was a victory of a kind. A hope for a new day, a new world.

The Ghetto had a promenade, which stretched along the north side of Leszno Street between Nalewki and Karmelicka Streets. There, during the afternoon and early evening, teenage girls and boys replayed the ageless traditions of the ever-adaptive mating game. Walking past each other as they pounded the sidewalks in opposite directions, they searched for signs of mutual attraction through eye contact. Without speaking to each other, they seemed to be trying to find the presence or absence of compatibility before taking any chances. Bolek and I hadn't yet reached that stage, but we enjoyed observing what we considered to be their ridiculous behaviour. Occasionally, we played a parody of it with girls our age or older. We vocalised and jostled more than the mature Romeos and Juliets. We were very much surprised when we appeared to be taken seriously by some of the girls.

The promenade ceased to function as a meeting place sometime in the autumn of 1940, before we moved from our apartment on Mirowska Street. Since Bolek and his parents moved at the same time, I only saw him once at his new location, a one-room lodging on Twarda Street. I saw his parents, who smiled proudly when Bolek's voice—in the process of change—cracked and alternated between highs and lows as he spoke. That was the last time I ever laid eyes on my best friend, Bolek Grynszpan.

The worst was yet to come, though. In the middle of July 1942, another part of the Ghetto, including our present location on Gesia Street, was cut away. We had to move again. This time, to Aunt Dwora's on Nowolipie Street.

Aunt Dwora and her husband owned a shoemakers' supply store. A youngish-looking woman, she was the mother of four boys aged between fifteen and twenty. All of her boys were working in factories, two of the younger ones in shoe factories, the oldest son in metallurgical works, and the middle one in a sugar refinery. No sooner had my mother, my brother, and I settled in Aunt Dwora's kitchen, which was the only available room, than the Germans threw their last card on the table. With the help of their Ukrainian and Latvian henchmen, they started the liquidation of the

Warsaw Ghetto. On July 22, 1942, yellow sheets of paper pasted on walls proclaimed that "All Jews living in the Warsaw Ghetto (except those working in German-approved industries such as making uniforms and shoes, and their immediate families), will be repatriated to another city somewhere beyond a certain river."

It urged all the non-exempt population to report to the assembly point, or *Umschlagplatz*, at the corner of Zamenhofa and Niska.

The following day, another announcement was posted on walls of the Ghetto. It was smaller, on white paper, and it had a black border. It read: "Mr. Adam Czerniakow, Chairman of the Jewish Council, died. He died by his own hand, of poisoning."

Simultaneously, German trucks appeared on the streets. Armed Germans and their stooges dressed in German uniforms started to round up men, women, and children from streets and from their homes, killing and stealing as they went along. Only those people who had stamped documents testifying to their usefulness to the Germans were released. But even some of these were not so lucky.

Some of the Latvians and Ukrainians—the scum of their own people—couldn't read. The Jews had their own share of scum: Jewish policemen who helped deport their own parents to please their German masters and believed they were safe because they were useful. My mother continued to go about her business of providing food for her children. She obtained some from CENTOS. She was carrying an identity card attesting to the fact that she worked for the organization. She hoped that it would be recognized should she be picked up from the street. But it wasn't.

It wasn't.

On the day that was to be the saddest of my life, I was home with Jerzyk, waiting for Mother to return with some food. There was a knock on the door. It was a man I knew, with a note from my mother written hastily on a crumpled scrap of paper. The man told me how the Germans were rounding up people on his street and forcing them to climb into a truck. He himself managed to stay hidden in a doorway, where the Germans didn't see him, but my mother did. She was one of the first to be caught. As soon as she saw him, she took a pencil and paper from her purse, and while the Germans were rounding up others, she hurriedly wrote the note, crumpled it, and threw it on the sidewalk where she was sure that he could see it. When the Germans left with the truck filled with people, he picked up the note and thought it was his duty to deliver it. He finally departed, his head bowed, telling us how sorry he was.

In the note, Mother instructed me to go to an address she had written down and ask a Jewish police officer named Kazimierski to free her.

I left Jerzyk in Aunt Dwora's care and ran all the way, dodging several German trucks. Officer Kazimierski, a tall, handsome man, was home with his wife and three-year-old daughter. He listened with concern and promised to do everything in his power to free my mother. Apparently, he had been a beneficiary of my mother's pre-war philanthropic activities. He had been an excellent student in the last year of high school, but his parents could not afford university tuition. My mother arranged a stipend grant, which gave him the means to achieve a master's degree. Hence, he was now a high-ranking member of the Jewish police. He suggested that until my mother's return, Jerzyk should be placed in an orphanage, directed by a man named Janusz Korczak, who could be called a saint, were he not Jewish. His real name was Henry Goldszmit.

Officer Kazimierski accompanied me home and spoke to Aunt Dwora. He took me and Jerzyk to Mr. Korczak's home, which housed two hundred children, where he arranged for Jerzyk's temporary stay.

While awaiting my mother's return, I visited my old friends at Hashomer Hatzair. They had moved from Gesia Street. Their new location on Nowolipki Street was disguised as a tailor shop. About twenty industrial sewing machines were being installed in two rows as I entered the large room. I was approached by two of the older members, who told me that there might be a job for me delivering notes to all the apartment caretakers. They said that they were getting organized for what they very vaguely explained as "more co-operation among the Jewish people."

They gave me some coupons redeemable for food at another location and told me to come back in three days. Early next morning, I went to redeem the coupons. As I was about to go back home after receiving the food, I heard a commotion. People were running up the stairs. Someone shouted: "The Germans are coming! The whole block is surrounded by trucks! Soldiers are getting out!"

The "blockade" became a daily occurrence in the Ghetto, but this was the first time I found myself in the midst of it. I saw that some of the people were climbing up the stairs, and I followed them. Once on the top floor, the first man to reach the end of the stairs picked up a ladder from the floor and leaned it against the wall. He quickly climbed up and pushed open a small trapdoor in the ceiling above. Then he climbed in and motioned to the others to follow. Everyone did. Men, already on top, helped to pull in the men and women still climbing up the ladder. The ladder was pulled up and the trapdoor tightly shut. This was the loft, the space under the roof of the five-storey building. It was dark and dusty. The small windows admitted only narrow, sharply defined light beams, which exposed myriad dancing particles of dust.

The people were spread out. Motionless. Each huddled in a dark place. It was quiet. But not for long. Wild screams of soldiers shouting in German, Ukrainian, and Latvian soon filled the building below. Carbine shots and cries of people could be heard. And the sounds of heavy boots—coming closer and closer. A few soldiers were now on the top floor. They spoke loud words to each other and went down the stairs again, the shuffle of their boots retreating farther and farther away. They left the building. Then the sound of trucks pulling away—and quiet at last. The people began to stir uncertainly in the dark places of the attic. Then one man got up and opened the trapdoor. A woman with a baby in her arms removed the handkerchief from her child's mouth. A girl of perhaps sixteen pulled down her summer dress from her hips, held there by her boyfriend's hand. In times of extreme crisis, people tend to cling to each other.

The people started to move towards the trapdoor, then climbed down the ladder one at a time. Still too stunned to talk aloud, they spoke in whispers. Only the baby gave vent to its natural feelings and screamed at the top of its voice. On my way down, I saw the body of a man lying on the floor. His brain was splattered on the wall. A few people stood around the crumpled remains of what had been a man just a few minutes before. The pinkish mass on the wall above spread in the form of a half circle, marking the man's height when he was still on his feet. One of the watchers said: "His brother-in-law is a Jewish police officer named Kazimierski. He was here already. Took one look and went out again."

I stood transfixed. "How did it happen?"

"He was killed by a Latvian," answered the same man. "The swine took him aside, against this wall, and demanded diamonds. The man kept telling him that he didn't have any gold or diamonds. Then he shot him."

I walked away wordlessly. On the street in front of the building stood Kazimierski. I walked over to him and looked up at his face. Something in his drained expression made me feel compassion towards him. Something within me made me speak out. "There's such emptiness all around us," I said. Kazimierski put his hand on my shoulder and said nothing. He looked at my face searchingly, as if seeing me for the first time. He withdrew his hand gently and started to walk towards the building gate.

I still held tightly to the small bundle of food under my arm. I now resumed my interrupted journey home. After eating some of it, I took out my bicycle so I could take some to my brother. On my way to the orphanage, I met a boy I knew from the choir. His family had been moved to Poland from Germany. The boy used to tell us fantastic stories about crossing borders: the searching for gold in people's rectums by the German police, and jokes about different German accents. The boy waved, and I stopped in front of him.

"Let me have a ride," said the boy. Before I could say anything, he said, "My father was taken away."

I looked at him. "What do you want a ride for?" I asked, taken aback by the incompatibility of the statements.

"Yes, what for?" echoed the boy, and stood there forlornly, a child lost in cruel realities.

As I approached the Janusz Korczak Orphanage, I saw people running in and out. I pressed on the pedals, my heart pounding. The door was open wide and children's clothing was scattered on the sidewalk. I ran into the house, screaming my brother's name. The house was empty. I rushed into the street and asked the first man I saw, "What happened? Where are the children?"

The man told me, "The whole house has been evacuated. They left a short while back. Janusz Korczak and all his staff went along with the children."

Almost out of my mind, I rushed to Officer Kazimierski's place. I opened the door, and there, sitting on the kitchen table eating a slice of cooked red beet, was Jerzyk! I laughed and cried and laughed again, as I hugged and kissed my brother, who looked surprised, not knowing what the fuss was all about. When I got hold of myself, Kazimierski told me how, while still in the apartment where his brother-in-law was shot, he received information through one of his men that the Janusz Korczak Orphanage was going to be evacuated by the Germans. He got there just one minute before the Germans did, snatched my brother out, and brought him home.

Then Kazimierski told me that his efforts to free our mother had failed. She was probably on the way to her destination right at that time. He told me not to worry. She would be all right, he said. Then he told me that he had a plan for me and for Jerzyk.

"You don't look like a Jew," he said. "If I can get you out of the Ghetto, you'll have a good chance of passing as a Pole and survive the war, living like a human being."

"But what about Jerzyk?" I asked. "Isn't he going out of the Ghetto with me?"

"No," answered Kazimierski firmly. "I will make arrangements for him to stay with your aunt Dwora as her own son. I will make papers for him, and he will be all right.

You will all meet after the war is over. A small child like him does not understand. If he went along with you, he would give himself, and you, away. Then you would both be dead."

Reassured by Kazimierski of the fact that since all four of Aunt Dwora's sons were working, she had the right to stay in the Ghetto and would not be bothered by the Germans, I agreed to the plan.

Kazimierski took us to Aunt Dwora and explained his plan to her. She listened to Kazimierski, and after hearing that there was no chance of bringing our mother back, agreed to take care of Jerzyk if the papers could be arranged and ration cards provided for him as her son. Kazimierski assured her that he would take care of it himself. As for me, I would seek refuge with one of my mother's old friends outside the Ghetto. I was told to come to Kazimierski's house the next morning, at five o'clock sharp.

I slept badly that night. A nightmare kept returning every time I fell asleep. It repeated a terrible scene I had witnessed about a year earlier at the Ghetto outlet of Zelazna and Leszno Streets. A gendarme was beating a Jewish passerby with a black rubber bludgeon. The man begged for mercy, but in vain. The bludgeon came down again and again on the victim's bald head. He covered his head with his hands, only to receive the merciless barrage of cruel blows on his fingers, hands, wrists. I woke up before the man passed out and collapsed to the cold sidewalk. I went back to troubled sleep, only to wake up again. I knew that it was the fear and anticipation of the next day's ordeal, and the worry about Jerzyk, both combined, that recreated this inhuman scene in my mind.

When I woke up at four o'clock in the morning, I kissed Jerzyk and said good-bye quietly so as not to start him crying. I emptied my pockets of all change and gave it to my brother, which made the child happy. My uncle and two younger cousins were still asleep. I embraced my crying Aunt Dwora and shook hands with the older cousins, who wished me good luck. All the way to Kazimierski's house I wondered whether I was doing the right thing in leaving my brother.

Officer Kazimierski of the Jewish Warsaw Ghetto Police, wearing his three official armbands (one identifying him as a resident of the Warsaw Ghetto, one as a Jewish policeman, and one as an officer) waited for me at his apartment. We went out into the street, and Kazimierski motioned to a passing rickshaw driver. The driver, wearily pushing at his converted three-wheeler's pedals, grudgingly obliged, as he thought that he would not get paid by a policeman. He didn't. We disembarked near the junction of Leszno and Zelazna Streets.

I was carrying a small bundle containing three shirts, two pairs of socks, and some underwear. I was wearing an oversized checkered pair of pants, a grey sports jacket, a pair of brown shoes too large for me (as they used to belong to my father), and a navy blue gymnasium regulation coat. My parents bought it for me after I completed public school. It used to have shiny nickel buttons and light blue stripes on the sleeves, but the Germans forbade these things, so the shiny buttons were replaced by plain black ones and the stripes were darkened with black ink.

We walked into the doorway of an apartment building. Kazimierski questioned some people. I couldn't hear what about, but I heard their answers. They told him that getting out of the Ghetto with a parcel in one's hands was impossible. Not that getting out at all was easy. I undressed in the doorway, put all my shirts on, one on top of the other, then put my coat back on. Kazimierski waited in front of the building until I was ready. He then motioned to me to cross the street.

"You go first," he said.

A work battalion of fifty men was approaching. The Jewish men were marching five to a row, right down the middle of Leszno Street. The approach of the first row of men coincided with my crossing the street, and the man on the extreme left of the first row, while marching, pushed me out of the way. In a split second, Kazimierski was there in front of the man, and while I looked on with incomprehension at the spectacle before my eyes, Kazimierski slapped the man across the face with the open palm of his hand. It was only much, much later that I understood the motives of Kazimierski's action. He wanted the marching men to know without a doubt that he was my protector. It was imperative to his plan for my escape from the Warsaw Ghetto.

This outlet of the Warsaw Ghetto looked as follows: Zelazna Street was divided straight in the middle by the three-metre brick Ghetto wall. There was a two-lane-wide opening, intersected by Leszno Street. The work battalion was now marching along Leszno Street, towards the opening. On each side of the opening was a black-,red-, and white-striped sentry booth. In front of each sentry booth stood a tall, green-uniformed German *Schutzpolizist* wearing shiny metal ornaments on his chest and helmet. Beside each German stood a blue-uniformed Polish policeman and a Jewish policeman.

Men in the work battalion were being searched by the Germans and the Polish policemen to make sure that they weren't taking any valuables out of the Ghetto. Things such as gold and diamonds were worth a lot more on the Aryan side. The work battalions were led out of the Ghetto each morning under armed civilian guard to perform heavy labour outside the Ghetto and brought back in at the end of each day. While the search was in progress, Officer Kazimierski and I, keeping close to the Ghetto wall, approached the Jewish policeman, who was standing near the sentry booth on the right. He perked up when he saw his superior. "Get this boy out of the Ghetto," said Kazimierski. The man nodded. Kazimierski left.

I stood beside the sentry booth with my back pressed tightly against the Ghetto wall. I was out of sight of the Germans and the Polish police who were still searching the men in the work battalion.

The Jewish policeman turned his face slightly towards me. "Listen," he said, "when I give you a signal like this"—

he twisted his right hand at the wrist behind his back—"you throw down your armband and mix with the men." He motioned to the work battalion with his chin. "If they catch you"—he paused—"you don't know me. Understand?"

I nodded.

My heart was pounding through my back against the brick and concrete of the Ghetto wall. With my left hand, I loosened the band with the blue Star of David on my right arm. I waited...

Then it happened. The signal. The armband slid off easily. A few quick steps, and I found myself between two rows of marching men at the back of the work battalion. They kept pushing me away, fearing for their lives. But they remained silent. Their feet were kicking me as they pretended that I wasn't there. I couldn't stand the pushing and kicking much longer.

Now! I jumped over to the sidewalk and kept walking. My mind buzzed. Don't look back!

I didn't.

# part two

---

EVERY STEP CARRIED ME FARTHER AND FARTHER FROM THE
Ghetto walls. At first, when I was only ten paces beyond the
German gendarmes and Polish police at the outlet of the
Ghetto, I walked stiffly, my mind frozen in dread of hear-
ing "Halt!" shouted at me at any moment.

The shout did not come! I kept on walking, trying to
occupy my mind with anything far removed from my immediate situation. The windows of the adjacent apartment
buildings had been cemented over with recycled bricks. I
concentrated on the number of steps it took me to walk from
one window to the next. My body, taut at first, became more
relaxed with each step. The rapid beat of my heart gradually gave way to a warmth that spread through my breast. I
took a long, deep breath, and all of a sudden, I felt good.

The name of the street stretching before me was Leszno.

I knew the route well because of the long walks Bolek and I used to take through the city. I remembered that farther up the street was a huge, open market square called Kiercelak, officially known as Plac Kercelego, on the left between Leszno and Chlodna Streets.

Almost anything could be bought or sold there. There were hundreds of tiny wooden stalls, a maze of passages and white-painted booths, and crowds of people. Farmers brought their produce and sold it straight off the wagons, while their horses munched from burlap feed bags. And, I remembered, there were some booths where a hungry customer could buy a chunk of mouth-watering kielbasa, piled in fragrant coils on the counter next to baskets of fresh kaiser buns. Or rye breads with caraway seeds protruding from their shiny, golden crusts. I realized that I was hungry, very hungry. I had hardly eaten anything during the past three days, and had left my brother most of the food I'd received from Hashomer Hatzair.

Jerzyk... If only he could have come with me. Maybe I could still get him out... But then, if we got caught, we would both be killed. No, it's better this way. Kazimierski promised that he would take care of everything. At least he'll be relatively safe. If I live through it all, we'll meet after the war. These thoughts swirled through my head. Who knows what lies ahead of me? Why should a small child like Jerzyk be forced to live a day-to-day existence, dodging the Germans? My mind told me that I was right, but my heart was in turmoil.

When I reached the marketplace, I found that it hadn't changed. The booths were still there, just as before. I approached the nearest food stall and ordered a loaf of dark rye bread and a kilo of kielbasa. Then I sat down on a narrow bench in front of the counter and devoured the food. I watched the vendor, a fat woman wearing a white kerchief and a matching apron, pour a glass of vodka for a customer from a clear wine bottle, after a quick, cautious glance around the stall. It was homemade, black-market vodka known as *bimber*. "Can I buy a glass of that, too?" I asked. The woman took one indifferent look at me and poured a glassful. I drained the glass in a single, uninterrupted motion. It burned my throat, but it made me feel better. I paid her, slid off the bench, and left the stall.

The sun was coming up. I wore my blue winter coat on top of a jacket, plus three shirts underneath. As I walked past the square, I realized that I was approaching two German-occupied office buildings, clearly identified by swastikas on flags hanging at a threatening angle flanking the entrances. I felt a sudden pang of fear. Do I look conspicuous? Will they notice my heavy winter coat (this was August) or my pale, thin face? And my eyes...do I look scared? I saw a uniformed German guard in front of a building. Two German soldiers were walking on the sidewalk towards me. Simultaneously, I saw a street vendor selling sunflower seeds in little paper bags in a box suspended from his neck.

I bought a bag and started to eat the seeds, spitting the

empty shells onto the sidewalk. I swung my body noncha-
lantly, as any *cfaniak* (wiseguy) in Warsaw would, and I
began to whistle—when not splitting shells with my teeth.
They didn't notice me. They looked right past me! My self-
confidence restored, I walked on towards my destination.

Novogrodzka was the street where my mother's friends
lived. I had to reconstruct in my mind, from visits going
back at least three years, the sight of the apartment building and the correct floor. They were a middle-class Polish
family named Palmowski. My mother taught piano to their
talented daughter. I had met them twice before. Once, on
a Christmas Eve, to help decorate the tree in their living
room. Another time, when my mother took me along on a
shopping spree with Mrs. Palmowska at Warsaw's largest
department store, Jablkowski Brothers. Their friendship
had been that of intellectual, cultural, and financially secure
equals. They liked and respected one another.

I recognized the exterior of the five-storey apartment
building, and almost at once recalled that the Palmowskis'
six-room apartment was on the second floor. I walked
through the doorway, climbed two marble flights of stairs,
and knocked on the door. It was too early in the morning
to ring the bell. The sound of footsteps approached.

A woman's voice asked tersely, "Yes? Who is it?"

"The son of Mrs. Schaller," I whispered into the key-
hole.

The lock clicked and the door opened just a crack at
first, then wide. A woman's hand reached out of the dark-

ness and, taking hold of my arm, pulled me into the entrance hall. The door shut behind me.

"How is she?" asked Mrs. Polmowska, speaking of my mother. "Where have you been all this time?" While she was asking all kinds of questions, her husband came out of the bedroom, and I told them both as much as possible of what had happened to us. While I talked, they led me into the living room, and then sat listening in silence. Their faces expressed concern, anger, and fear in turn. But most of their expressions reflected shocked disbelief. As my descriptions of various aspects of life in the Ghetto unfolded before them, the words coming out of my mouth clashed with their elegant surroundings. I felt a sense of unreality as I spoke to this middle-aged couple, sitting in their dressing gowns, which still seemed to emanate an air of warm, comfortable sleep.

When I stopped at last, they in turn attempted to recount what the Germans were doing to the Aryan Polish people. It sounded like small-town gossip in comparison to what I had seen in the Ghetto. They sensed my feelings, and made short end of their tales.

"The first thing we will do is give you a bath," said Mrs. Palmowska. She took me by the hand and led me into the kitchen, where she filled a washtub with warm water from the sink and told me to undress and get into it. Then she left the kitchen.

Just as I was about to sit down in the tub, she returned to the kitchen. I was deeply embarrassed. Not only because of my nakedness, but also because I had red malnutrition sores on my upper legs. I tried to explain that the sores were caused by scurvy, which resulted from lack of vitamin C in the Ghetto diet. My explanation fell on deaf ears. It became obvious to me that my penis, not my health, was her focus of concern.

I had been wondering why Mrs. Palmowska had gone to the trouble of filling a washtub in the kitchen, when I knew from previous visits that there was a modern four-piece bathroom in their apartment. The answer came to me in a sudden flash. She wanted to see if my circumcision was evident at a glance. She had probably never seen a circumcised male, and wanted to see if it would be possible to deny my Jewishness were I caught by the Germans. Once I understood her motives in setting up this "observation opportunity," my embarrassment vanished. This was a question of life or death for them and for myself.

The following two weeks, I lived in what seemed an earthly paradise. Good food, and plenty of it. A bath every day. Peaceful leisure between meals, spent playing their fine baby grand piano and reading books and magazines. A comfortable bed to sleep in. After years of deprivation, this truly was paradise. I approached my host about Jerzyk. "Could it be arranged to try to get him out of the Ghetto, with Kazimierski's help?" I pleaded with them.

They answered negatively, their faces stiff with fear. "Too risky. He is too small. He might talk and give himself away to the Germans. Besides," they said, "who is crazy enough to start a negotiation through a third person, about getting a Jewish child out of the Ghetto? If it leaked out, everyone would be killed—the whole family."

As time went on, I sensed how afraid they were of being caught with me, a Jew, in their apartment. I could not blame them. Their recently married daughter, who occupied two rooms of their spacious apartment, was pregnant. As for themselves, who doesn't want to live?

One day, when the whole family was gathered for dinner, I spoke up. I thanked them for their hospitality and kindness. I said I appreciated it very much, but I had to leave.

They protested, but I could see that they were relieved. "Where will you go? What will you do?" they asked.

"I'll go to the countryside and look for work on a farm. My being here is too dangerous for you—as well as for me," I said. "I'll walk to the west," I explained, "towards Wola." I'd travelled there before, on my bicycle, when I was nine or ten, so I had a picture of the area in my mind.

"At the far side of Wola, the last streetcar stop is called Kolo. If I continue walking west, I should reach a belt of vegetable and fruit farms. I'll look for work there." Everyone agreed that this was a good plan.

Mr. Palmowski suggested that I should be given a haircut. He promised to take me to a barber, because my long hair made me conspicuous. I felt that no matter what the consequences, I had made the right decision in leaving this kind family and freeing them of their fears.

The next morning, Mrs. Palmowska helped me to pack my few shirts and pieces of underwear, all freshly laundered, in a neat little bundle. I said good-bye to her and her daughter and son-in-law, and left the house with Mr. Palmowski for a nearby barbershop. While I was getting my long-overdue haircut, he stood guard quietly in front of the shop. Afterwards, we shook hands, and Mr. Palmowski wished me luck. Then we parted, each going a different way.

I reached the first farm village by late afternoon, walking all the way, and without any trouble. I passed the first farm, and the second. The third farm looked right to me, and I walked in. I was hired as a tomato picker. I had a warm meal and lodging for the night.

Not being familiar with Catholic songs, I found, could be very dangerous for me. Other boys working in the fields with me were singing a song that repeated what seemed to be its title, "Santa Lucia," with each refrain. I didn't know the words, and kept silent. A couple of the boys began to ask questions, jokingly, but full of spite and serious underneath. "Have you ever been across the border?" they asked. "Were there high walls on the frontier?" I managed to confuse them by talking about towns and places in Poland that I'd visited before the war. At day's end, they weren't sure if I was a Jew. The job lasted only two days, most of the ripe tomatoes having already been picked. I was relieved when the farmer told me the following evening that he would have to let me go.

On I went, the next morning, with the 20 zlotys earned for the two days' work. After passing two villages, I came to a place called Otarzew. There, I saw a large colonial country estate house surrounded by a flower garden. An intelligent-looking older couple sat on a bench in front of the house. I walked over to them and asked for a job. I got it.

They liked my clear city accent and polite manner. Their name was Dahlen. He was a man over fifty, of medium height, with sparse hair and a reddish complexion. He had good posture in spite of his corpulence, which was not surprising, since he was a retired colonel from the Polish army. His wife was slightly taller than he, and slimmer, but not thin. She had very fine features, delicate and strong at the same time. There was something in her face that reminded me of my mother. They wanted to know my name and background, and I told them my name was Arthur Szalewski (so as not to forget my assumed name, I chose Szalewski, which sounded similar in Polish to Schaller). I told them that my father was in Russia, my mother was in jail for smuggling, and my brother was in Warsaw with an aunt. (I didn't mention that it was in the Ghetto.) Lying wasn't easy when dealing with such kind people, but there was no other way if I were to survive. I wasn't used to it at all. As it turned out later, I was a poor liar anyway.

My job was to take Dahlens' three cows to the pastures every morning, watch them so they didn't wander off into the fields, and bring them back to the cowshed at night. It was pleasant enough. I lay on my back, looking at the blue sky, glancing at the grazing cows once in a while. But this pastoral existence was not meant to last. One morning, Mrs. Dahlen came to see me while I was in the pastures.

She said, "Arthur, I am going to Warsaw on business today, and I think it would be wise to change your registration with the police. Tell me, what is your aunt's address? I will go over to her place, and get your papers from her."

I tried to talk her out of it, but I didn't have any valid excuse to back up my argument. Every Pole had to have a slip of paper from the Polish police, as proof that he had registered his place of residence. This was something everyone had to do, even before the German occupation. Suddenly, Mrs. Dahlen said, "Tell me the truth, Arthur, are you a Jew?"

I had a strange feeling of despair and relief. I rejected the despair, and my honesty and faith in human nature and in myself took over. Only seconds passed between the unexpected question and my answer, but I was calm and composed when I answered with pride, "Yes, I am a Jew."

I looked at her face and read a confirmation of my belief—there was compassion in it. "I am glad you told me the truth," said Mrs. Dahlen. "It will be a secret between us, and I will try to help you all I can."

She kept her word. Two days passed, and not even her husband knew my real identity. On the third day, she came and handed me a little black booklet. She said, "This is a book of Catholic prayers and songs. If you learn the prayers and songs, it may help you pass as a Catholic. Please take it."

I took the booklet and thanked her for it. When she left, I started to leaf through it, then I read it from beginning to end, again and again. By the end of the week, I had memorized it. I knew all the common prayers: "Our Father," "Hail, Mary," "I Believe," and so on. I knew prayers to saints, and a prayer to one's own personal angel, as well as about a dozen songs—word for word. I had the opportunity to practice the songs, as a group of women working in a nearby field sang together every day, and I sang along with them as I watched the cows.

The Dahlens had a son my age, and we soon became good friends, walking around the estate and talking about many things. His name was Janek. He was taller than I, and also more naive. He had a proud, patriotic upbringing and constantly discussed ways to throw the Germans out of Poland. He often spoke of weapons and different strategies he had learned about from his father.

Winter was drawing nearer—it was the beginning of October 1942. I had spent at least three weeks at the Dahlen estate in Otarzew, and I was getting used to the daily routine. I heard talk about Germans encountering ever-growing Russian resistance in Stalingrad, but when I got hold of a copy of the *New Warsaw Courier*, now German controlled, all the items dealing with battles on the Russian front seemed to indicate that the Germans were victorious. One could read about "strategic retreats" and "straightening of lines." Never was there any indication that the Germans were being pushed back out of Russia, as the people were secretly saying. Sometimes, after overhearing talk of the Germans losing the war, I dreamed of seeing my parents and my brother again. Returning to reality, I felt more lonely than ever.

If only I had an instrument, I thought, a musical instrument of any kind, I would learn to play it. I tried making flutes out of willow branches—stripping the bark and drying it, fashioning a reed—but they didn't produce satisfactory sound. Singing was the only outlet for my musical yearning, and I sang often.

Mrs. Dahlen came to see me again in the pastures. I looked at her face, and read fear in it. She said, "I have bad news, Arthur. We have received notice from the German military authorities that they are sending some German soldiers to quarter on our estate. I had to tell my husband about you. It came as quite a shock to him."

She stopped for a moment, as if to give me time to prepare myself for what was coming. "We had a long discussion. This is a serious situation. The lives of all of us are involved. If the Germans found out who you are, they could kill us all. We have a son your age. Do you understand?"

I felt numb and tired. "Yes, I understand," I said. "I'll leave tomorrow." That evening, Janek and I took our usual walk through the estate. Janek joked about my brown sport shoes, worn by now, which, being my father's shoes, were too large for my feet. When we came back from our walk, I was given a pair of wooden clogs by Mrs. Dahlen, to help me save what was left of my father's leather shoes. Janek was told I was leaving, but not why I had to leave. He was told, however, that the Germans were coming to live on the estate, and went about enthusiastically preparing plans to blow them up.

I left the estate early the next morning, going...who

knew where? But still in the same direction—away from Warsaw.

A village appeared in the distance, the gleaming white-washed homes standing out against the slanted outlines of thatched roofs. My heart beating, I selected a farmhouse. One man and two women were winnowing wheat. A woman in a red smock was pouring grain from a burlap bag into the top of a hand-operated winnowing machine. The other woman collected the purified grain, and the man turned the handle. The air was full of dust, chaff, and noise. I was hired for two days' work, to take over the man's job. I wasn't really strong enough for the job, and after the first day of pressing the wooden handle, my hands were covered with painful blisters.

I didn't complain when the farmer handed me a ten zloty note instead of twenty, as we'd agreed, after two days' work. And again I walked the dirt road.

Walking at night was dangerous because of Germans posted in fields after nightfall, guarding the stacks of har-vested grain against sabotage. But it was equally or even more dangerous to sleep in the open, or in the ditches. So I found ways of burrowing into a haystack, making a nest inside. I kept my coat on and curled up into a ball, as the nights were getting cold. At daylight, I would emerge and look for a stream or a well, where I could wash and have a drink of water. For food, I scavenged whatever I could find in the fields, mostly carrots and some apples. It was at one such "lunch stop" that I met Mr. Bargiel. I was sitting at the edge of a country road scraping a carrot with my pocket knife when a wagon rigged for hauling grain came roaring by. Two long wooden boards formed the floor of the wagon, and a wooden ladder ran along each side. "Whoa!" yelled the driver at the horses, and the wagon came to a slow stop in a cloud of dust.

"Where you going, boy?" the driver hollered at me.

"I'm looking for work." I answered, as I got up and started to walk towards the wagon.

"Hop on," said the driver. I did. The man shook the reins, shouted at the horses, and the wagon took off with a jerk. I held on to one of the ladders with one hand and held my bundle tightly in the other, assessing the new situation. I took a close look at the driver. He was a burly Polish farmer, big, red-faced, and mustached. He was standing like a Roman gladiator, his legs wide apart, the reins in both hands, looking straight ahead without saying anything to me. I was beginning to wonder if he was taking me to the Polish police, who were just as bad as the Germans to whom they swore loyalty. I thought, If I see anything suspicious, I'll jump off and roll over on the ground a few times before I start running.

We reached a very small town called Leszno. The driver slowed down a bit, but kept going. I noticed a German gendarme post, the windows protected by steel blinds. I got ready to escape at any sign of the driver stopping or slowing down. He kept going, and soon passed through Leszno. After five more kilometres, we arrived at a village named Grzadki, according to the signpost.

The wagon turned left into an open gate, leading into a yard, and came to a slow stop. "Whoa!" bellowed the driver at his horses, as he wrapped the reins around the end of a ladder and jumped off the wagon. The yard was enclosed by a whitewashed house, a cowshed and stable, and an unpainted barn and toolshed. The buildings were one storey and had thatched roofs. I followed the driver into the house, where I saw a woman, about sixty, sitting on a chair in a whitewashed kitchen. She looked me over matter-of-factly, and shifted her eyes to the man, searchingly.

"Mother," said the man, "I brought you a boy, to help you out." "Boy"—he turned to me—"what's your name?"

"Joziek," I answered, "Joseph Szalewski."

I was a little surprised at myself. The change in my first name was not planned. It just slipped out while I was standing there, picturing the woman hollering "Arthur! Take out the cows!" It just wasn't the right kind of name to go with the cows. Might get me into trouble. The man faced me and said, "I need someone to help my mother with the chores. I live on my other farm—she is here by herself." He paused and then asked, "How much do you want a month? The work isn't hard, and you get your room and board."

"If you provide my clothes, that will be my pay," I replied.

"Good. You're hired," said the man, obviously satisfied with this arrangement. "By the way, where are you from? Where does your family live?" he wanted to know.

"I have no family. I'm an orphan," I answered, and then

continued: "My mother died before the war, and my father, who was a metal grinder, was killed in the Warsaw bombardment of 1939. I was left alone, and people told me that if I went into the countryside, I could making a living as a cowherd, so I did. All the papers were destroyed in a fire during the bombardment. I haven't any documents."

"Have you any other family?" asked the man.

"Not here. My mother and father came to Warsaw from Vilno, when I was a year old. I do have some family there, from my mother's side. Their name is Rybicki." I chose Vilno because it was now in Russia.

"All right, then, Joziek, come with me and I will show you the cowshed and tell you what your chores are. All right, Mother?" he asked, turning towards the woman.

"All right, Frank," said the woman, looking pleased, and added, "While you're there, show him a spot in the cowshed where he can bed down."

She was a short, stout woman. Her hair was greying and done up in sparse, short curls. Her wide face and narrow lips gave her the look of a tough and determined person, but there was a spark of humour in her lively brown eyes.

When we stepped in front of the house, Frank told me that their name was Bargiel. His father had died two years before. After his death, the land was divided into two parcels of sixteen morgs each (two morgs = nearly one-half hectare), one going to his brother, Victor, with new buildings being erected, and the other to him.

His mother was to stay on his sixteen-morg farm for the

rest of her life while he lived on his other farm. He came only to work the ground and gather the crops, Frank explained. He opened the door of the cowshed, and I saw three black-and-white cows and two yearlings, one spotted and one all black. Pointing to a place near the door, he said, "You can sleep here." And he added, "You take care of the cows, chop the wood, and do what my mother tells you to do." With that, he left and went to the house for a moment, then drove away.

It felt good to have a place to stay! It was very timely, too—winter was just a few weeks off, and wandering outside and sleeping in the fields would be next to impossible, not to mention the problem of finding food. As I stood in front of the cowshed, a new feeling of security flowed through my whole being. I heard Mrs. Bargiel's voice calling, "Joziek!" I remained in my euphoric state a few moments longer, until a thought shot through my mind: Joziek! That's me!

Hurrying into the house, I found Mrs. Bargiel in the kitchen. She said, "Take the cows out to the field behind the barn, and while they're grazing, take a pitchfork out of the tool shed and throw a wagonload of dung out of the cowshed. Frank will need it for the field he's plowing over tomorrow. And throw down some fresh straw for the cows, and some for yourself to lie on."

"Yes, Mrs. Bargiel," I said, and went to it. The field behind the barn was fenced, so the cows didn't need watching. I closed the gate behind them and went to work on the dung. Later at night, as I lay on a bed of straw, listening to the sounds of animals breathing, the not-unpleasant smell of a cowshed in my nostrils, I reflected how lucky I was to have a home. That night, I fell asleep smiling.

Winter came, and my daily life became a set routine: feeding and watering the animals, chopping firewood, and doing chores for Mrs. Bargiel—until one week before Christmas, when the Bargiels had a party at their home. Some German gendarmes from Leszno were present, drinking heavily and singing into the early hours of the morning. I was careful and kept out of sight as much as possible. However, it turned out that the Bargiels had promised to give the gendarmes a chicken during their inebriation, and I was summoned the next morning to deliver it. I could not refuse without arousing suspicion.

I took the five-kilometre walk to the gendarme post in Leszno, carrying a live chicken in a basket. I knocked at the steel door and, when questioned about my business, announced the purpose of my visit into a small peephole. The door opened, and I was received with pleasure by five gendarmes clad in white longjohns inside the stronghold. When I left the post, I took a deep breath and released it slowly. I felt like a mouse who had just foiled the cat. It was a good feeling. I walked back home and went about my usual round of duties.

Mrs. Bargiel's other son, Victor, was our neighbour across the fence. He had two hired people helping him run his farm, a buxom milkmaid, and a heavyset labourer. These two were on very intimate terms and were quite open about their relationship.

Their names were Peter and Bronislawa. The day I delivered the chicken to the gendarmes, Peter came to chat and find out more about me. He was also eager to buy my red leather wallet. The conversation went something like this:

"I got some free time, Joziek, so I came over," said Peter, twiddling a crooked stick in his hands.

"Good," I answered with a polite smile, thinking that I'd better be cautious with this fellow.

"Have you ever fucked a girl?" asked Peter unexpectedly.

"No, I haven't," I replied.

Peter's expression brightened. He threw away the stick and rubbed his callused palms together, a faraway look on his reddish, unshaven face.

"I fuck Bronislawa every day—sometimes two, even three times a day," he announced with pride.

My own knowledge of the mechanics of copulation was limited and purely theoretical at that time. Peter's bold admission surprised me, but it also aroused my curiosity.

"Aren't you afraid of making her pregnant?" I asked, knowing that Peter and Bronislawa were unmarried.

"I pull 'him' out," Peter said, pointing to his crotch, "before..."

I was impressed with the simplicity and relative ease of his practice of birth control, and stored that knowledge away for future reference. "Peter!" Victor called out at this point, and Peter had to cut his visit short and reluctantly get back to work.

Victor was a milder-mannered person than his brother, Frank. He, too, was married and had two daughters, aged four and six. The girls visited their grandmother, Mrs. Bargiel, every Sunday, and I enjoyed playing with them. We made up little games using pencils, paper, and scissors. I looked forward to Sundays. I had less work on Sundays, mainly maintenance chores. I had the special privilege of washing the upper half of my body in the kitchen on Sundays, using a small basin set on a chair. On weekdays, I had to break the sheet of ice that formed on the water in the hollow log beside the well before removing my shirt for a quick wash. It was invigorating, to say the least. But since I wasn't given any soap, I never felt completely clean.

I still hadn't received any clothing from the Bargiels, and my own clothes were getting pretty worn, especially at the knees of my pants and the sleeves of my jacket. I had a needle and a small roll of red thread, and in my spare time I patched them as best I could in the warmth of the cowshed. I wore my blue coat during the day and used it as a blanket at night, and I used pieces of cardboard to cover the holes in the soles of my father's shoes. But things were going to get better, I hoped. The Bargiels had promised me some clothes for Christmas. Two days had passed since my walk to Leszno, and preparations for the holidays were underway.

A couple of days before Christmas, Frank Bargiel arrived to pick a turkey for his holiday table. It became apparent that one of the birds was missing. A search failed to reveal its presence, and the Bargiels were ready to suspect anybody. Frank approached me and asked threateningly, "Did you sell the turkey?"

I used the strongest argument I could think of to prove my innocence. It was a foolhardy thing to do, but I could not bear being accused of a crime I did not commit. I said: "I could not dare to steal your turkey because...I am a Jew." Frank's response to that was quick. The turkey was now forgotten. Here was a bigger problem. He grabbed me by my arms and pushed me through the open door of the empty stable, slammed the door shut, and locked it with a hook. Then he left.

I was in a state of panic. I looked around in desperation, seeking a way to escape. The roof! There was an opening in the ceiling above me, used for throwing down straw to the horses. It would allow me to cross over to the adjacent cowshed and jump down through a similar opening. If only I could reach it! I looked around for something to stand on. There was only one object in the stable: a long pitchfork stuck into the dung. I switched my attention to the door. The hook! I could try to pry it up from the inside. I grabbed the pitchfork and stuck one of its four sharp points between the door and the door frame. It worked! The hook was moving up! The door swung open and I took a step forward, but Frank Bargiel was towering above me, blocking my escape. He pushed me down with such force that I fell against the manger. I got up and took another run for the door, only to find that my strength was no match against Frank's.

"Listen," hissed Frank between his clenched teeth, "Stay there and listen, or I will kill you!" My back against the wall, I was trapped. They will deliver me to the Germans; they will kill me. How will they kill me? Will they shoot me? Or will they torture me first? The faces of my brother, mother, and father passed through my mind. I will never see them again, came the painful thought.

"We had a talk, Mother and I," Frank was saying, "We won't give you to the Germans." There was a spark of hope in me now. "But you're only going to work for your food. We're doing you a favour, you know, taking a chance in keeping you." I was back in control of myself and gave a sign of acknowledgement with my head. Frank left and likely thought it was good business to keep a cheap labourer. Besides, if they delivered me to the Germans, questions would be asked: How come the Jew stayed with them that long, without being questioned about his papers, identification? And the neighbours, they would talk. They would say the Bargiels turned me in for the reward. What was it that the Germans offered for a Jew? Oh, yes—one hundred cigarettes and a bottle of vodka.

I cried that night. I cried to the depths of my heart. I cried for those who did good and for those who did evil. It was as if something had broken within me, the shield I had built to protect myself from the cruel realities of hunger, injustice, and suffering. Perhaps most of all, injustice was hard to bear. Why should one human being be hunted by other human beings when he hadn't done them any wrong? I was curled up like a child in his mother's womb. My chin almost touching my knees, the sound of my sobbing accompanied by the breathing of sleeping animals. Gradually the crying subsided, and I fell asleep.

Another month passed. The Bargiels stuck to their second agreement, and gave me neither clothing nor shoes. The privilege of washing in warm water on Sundays was taken away. My food consisted of thin potato soup with a few pieces of carrot floating around and a slice of stale black bread. Never any meat. I became infested with lice. Lice in my hair, lice in my clothes, which I wore day and night since I was not given any blankets.

Then they caught the turkey thief. It was Victor Bargiel's hired man, Peter. He had stolen the bird, and his girlfriend, Bronislawa, had cooked it. They had enjoyed a secret, pre-Christmas feast. Mrs. Bargiel caught him trying to steal eggs, and he admitted everything when threatened with the loss of his job.

I found a friend, a young Jew who was the son of a local horse dealer. His father had been killed in front of his eyes. He told me that he had looked on from behind a tree while the Germans forced his father, at gunpoint, to walk into a deep swamp until he drowned.

We spoke no more about it. I sensed how sick my friend was with guilt and despair. I shared my bread with him and brought pails of water into the cowshed so he could wash

himself without being seen. Since he was known throughout the district, he could not stay long in one place. He wandered from one farm to another, always urged to keep going
by the frightened farmers. Lately, his heart had started to
give out. He often had to lie down, gasping for breath.
When his heart ached, my own heart was breaking, watching him. Here was a young man who was being destroyed
not only by others, but also by his own sense of guilt. He
could not forgive himself for not dying with his father.

He would show up once every week or two, looking
more like a dead man. The last time I saw him, he said he
was going to give himself up. I tried to talk him out of it,
but he didn't seem to hear me. His eyes were looking
through solid objects, not seeing them. He wasn't afraid of
death any more—to him it would be a release. He left, and
I never saw him again. His name was David, and he was
twenty-five years old.

Shortly after my being a Jew and Peter's thievery were
discovered, Peter approached me, asking if I would be interested in selling my red leather wallet, my only possession
of any value, and the safe holding place for a precious pho-
tograph of Jerzyk, taken when he was two years old, in 1939.

"I'll give you 10 zlotys," he proposed, with the air of a
player who holds a royal flush in a poker game. I sensed
that he and probably his girlfriend, Bronislawa, blamed me
for their being caught. That, plus their knowledge of my
being a Jew, gave them an ominous sense of power. A strong
hand indeed.

I removed the photo and handed him the wallet. "Take good care of it," I said, weary sadness flooding my heart. He paid, seemingly satisfied.

Later that day, Bronislawa entered the stable, where I was spreading fresh straw. The horses were out at the time. After a perfunctory greeting, she hopped up onto an empty manger and sank her ample rear into it. Humming to herself, she pulled her green checked skirt higher and higher, spreading her legs and rocking her upper body in a slow, deliberate motion. Her lower legs, which reminded me of a couple of giant bowling pins, were swinging to and fro and looked quite ridiculous. "You know," she cooed, "they spotted a Jewish couple in a ditch. They say they were really going at it." When I glanced up at her face, she smiled invitingly and rocked more vigorously. "Up and down, up and down.... Jews are really hot, aren't they?"

I didn't witness the rest of her exhibition, as I found an urgent reason to attend to other chores, leaving her sunk in the manger. The last sight I had of her that day was of her plump legs dangling from the manger, and her unlaced, half-open boots.

Echoes of news of German defeats on the Russian front started to reverberate throughout January 1943. A hired farm worker named Vieslaw, a handsome man with a good nature and good character, became my friend and the bearer of news. I listened with bated breath as Vieslaw quoted facts and figures of the battle of Stalingrad. "On February the second, the last German soldier gave up to the Russians! Two hundred thousand Germans were killed!" announced Vieslaw, slapping his hands together, as if smashing a pesky insect.

"Does that mean that the war will soon be over?"

Vieslaw became serious. He slowly turned his head in sad denial of my hope. "No, Joziek, it may take a very long time. The Germans are still sitting on half the world, but it's a beginning."

I knew that I was vulnerable, now that my true identity was known to a number of local people. I sought Vieslaw's advice as to my relative security in staying here as opposed to escaping and moving on to another village. Vieslaw was wise and cautious. "Wait till spring," he said, "No one will hire you in February—and besides, you'd freeze to death." I agreed, and decided to plan my escape as soon as the weather would permit. With hope, life was bearable. I resolved to play my submissive role cunningly. They would never suspect that I was planning to leave.

Mrs. Bargiel invited her thirteen-year-old niece to stay and keep her company. She was a thin, tall, plain-faced blond girl, who—having been informed that I was a Jew—looked at me with total incomprehension, as if I were a visitor from another planet. Her name was Teresa, and her presence, as it later turned out, was helpful in my eventual escape.

Perhaps it was my own entrance into puberty and my own growing awareness of sexuality that made me aware of the degree to which people around me were preoccupied with sex. Mrs. Bargiel began acting differently towards me.

She made a couple of statements to the effect that she, at fifty-five, was still a young woman, and would still be willing to engage in sex "with the right party." Then, a day later, she told me to sleep in an iron bed in the kitchen during the cold February nights.

I had barely curled up under a newly issued blanket, when she sent Teresa, who slept in the same room with her, into the kitchen to search for lice. The girl stood stark naked, holding a candle in one hand and her nightgown in the other, searching her body for lice. Naturally, my curiosity got the better of me a couple of times, and I peeked from under the blanket. I noticed that the girl had neither breasts nor pubic hair. I wondered at the purpose of Mrs. Bargiel's ordering this exhibition. Did she expect me to jump out of bed and ravish Teresa?

Whatever Mrs. Bargiel's expectations, when a week passed without any reaction to this "bait" on my part, I was unceremoniously ordered back to the cowshed and my blanket was confiscated. What followed was even more bizarre. No sooner had I settled down on the straw that first night back in the shed when Mrs. Bargiel barged in, lantern in hand, with an angry look on her face. She picked up a three-legged milking stool and tried to attack me with it. As she chased me around the shed, I concentrated my efforts on keeping my genitals covered, since I was wearing only a shirt. It was sheer terror! Only my youthful agility allowed me to frustrate her determination to see me exposed. In retrospect, I think that she wanted to find out if I was "the right party."

Mrs. Bargiel had a sister, also widowed, who came from Ciechanow to pay her a visit. In contrast with Mrs. Bargiel, she was a regular churchgoer and had a moderating influence on her sister. She sensed the vulnerability of my situation, and said to me quietly, "Do not leave this place. Death waits for you outside."

My feeling of insecurity grew into desperation with each passing day. Every night I would lie awake, listening to the breathing of cows and the clinking of chains tied around their necks. My body and hair became infested with lice. But even more aggravating, and more nagging than the bites of the lice, were my fears. Too many people knew my real identity. Far too many people, whose greed, hatred towards Jews, or the desire for some excitement made them potentially dangerous.

With mid-March came warmer weather, and some of the fields were being fertilized, plowed, and harrowed. Vieslaw arrived, bringing other men and women to help work in the fields. He cut a handsome figure in his riding britches, high, black boots, and curled mustache. So attractive was he to the opposite sex that they could not help staring when he walked ahead of them. One woman announced, "I wouldn't mind fucking him." He knew that he was attractive to women, but he chose to ignore it. There was, however, a love in his life. He told me about it during a lunch break.

"Her father is the *soltys* [reeve] of Stanislawow, about twenty kilometres from here," he said, his eyes looking dreamily into the distance. "I made love to her while her father sat right across the dinner table, and he knew nothing about it." He paused, while I marvelled at the technique that permitted him to practice this deception.

Our conversation turned to my own desperate situation, and it was at this point that Vieslaw exclaimed, "Say! That gives me an idea! You could go to the village of Stanislawow—to the *soltys*'s house. Ask him for work. You could tell him that I sent you, and you could give my greetings to him, and to her as well!" He added, "Her name is Maria." We agreed that when the time for my escape came, it would be my destination.

The opportunity came sooner than I expected. One week before the Easter Holiday, the Bargiels had a change of heart. They brought a man to cut my hair. The operation was performed with hand-operated, double-zero clippers while I sat on a milking stool in front of the cowshed. It left my head as bare as an egg. They also provided me with a pair of grey cotton britches, a shirt, and a grey pin-striped jacket. None of the clothes were new, but they were clean and undamaged. My old clothes were packed into a paper-thread bag and padlocked inside the toolshed. Soap was provided this time as well, and I scrubbed myself for an hour before putting on my new clothes. I hoped that the lice would stay away, and they did. I was clean again.

The morning of Easter Sunday, Mrs. Bargiel and Frank climbed on their wagon and drove away to another village to pay a visit to their relatives. The time was ripe for my escape. Teresa was in the kitchen preparing lunch. There was no one else on the farm. Still, I had to be careful. Victor Bargiel and his family were at their home just a loud shout away. If the girl were to notice that I was trying to leave, she would surely call for their help. I busied myself close to the toolshed.

I managed to lift the locked door of the toolshed off its hinges. Then I took out the basket containing my old clothes, and hung the door back as best I could. The clothes were old and worn, but they were my only possessions. I carried the basket into the barn, and hid it in a pile of straw.

Next, I applied my shoulders to a short wooden board at the rear wall of the barn. It took some pushing, but the nails on the bottom pulled out. I lifted the board and tried to crawl out on the other side. After getting out, I crawled back inside and pulled the board after myself, so it was not apparent that the board had been loosened. That done, I went into the house to eat my lunch.

My plate empty, I took Mrs. Dahlen's little black booklet out of my pocket, and proceeded to sing and recite psalms and prayers from it. When I finished praying, I turned to Teresa—who looked amazed at my passionate oratory to God—and asked politely: "May I have my piece of cake now? I'm still hungry."

"Yes, I guess so," replied the girl, still confused but unsuspecting.

"I'll go to the barn to have a little snooze." She nodded. Actually, I needed the cake as a travelling provision. Who could tell where my next meal would come from? In the barn, I wrapped the cake in a piece of paper, dug out my basket, and pushed out the loose board. I slipped out and kept walking straight ahead.

This being a fairly dry spring, the deep V-shaped culverts were dry. There was one running in just the same direction as I was walking, so I jumped into it and continued at a brisk pace. The culvert was as deep as I was high, so no one could see me now. This direction took me still farther away, west of Warsaw.

At nightfall, I reached a small village where a wedding was being celebrated. I walked into the pink-painted mud-brick house, where half of the village population was crowded into a large room with an earthen floor, eating and drinking. All of them were standing, as there was no room to sit down. When I appeared in the door, someone shouted: "Come on in, boy. Hey! Give the boy something to eat and drink!"

I was handed a slice of bread, a slice of headcheese, and a tall glass of beer. I consumed the offerings, thanked the man who gave me the food and drink, and left the house, gratefully recalling an old Polish saying in praise of hospitality that I had learned in school: Guest in house, God in house.

I passed through the quiet village at a quick pace, without stopping. It was still too close to the Bargiel farm, and I hoped to find lodging for the night. The fields were bare this early in April, and the night air was cold. Suddenly, the silhouette of a man holding a pitchfork appeared in the semi-darkness ahead. He seemed to be spreading manure over an unplowed field.

I tried to apply some reasoning before approaching him. His back was turned to me, and he had not yet seen me. Who would perform this kind of work at such a late hour on an Easter Sunday? Not a prosperous man, certainly. More than likely a poor man. A servant? No. Farmhands don't work in the fields during holidays. Therefore, a poor farmer with little land and no ability to pay for hired help, or a tenant farmer, even more strapped financially.

I took a calculated chance, approaching a stranger at this late hour. It was either that or being out all night in a strange, unknown district.

"Good evening, sir." I spoke softly so as not to startle the man.

"Jesus Christ, Holy Mary, Mother of God! Where are you coming from this time of night?" the man exclaimed.

I thought he spoke with a Warsaw accent, and I answered, "I'm an orphan from Warsaw, and am looking for lodging overnight."

"What's your name?" the man asked, leaning on his pitchfork. I could see his face in the moonlight now. It was the face of an educated man. He was short and wore a sleeveless padded jacket.

"My name is Joseph Szalewski. I'm looking for work."

"I could use some help," sighed the man, "if I could afford it. But you can stay overnight, and we'll see."

That night, I slept in the barn of, as I had guessed, the

tenant farmer. He would have kept me permanently, but hardly had enough food for his own family—a wife and two daughters. They had come from Warsaw for the sake of the children's health. Renting land halved their profits.

Still, he kept me on for three days, the next day being part of the Easter holiday. No work was done, and I stayed in the house. This day was called *Lany Poniedzialek*, or Splash Monday. Boys wait in hiding for the girls to pass by and then splash them with cupfuls, or even pails of water. The remaining two days, I worked in the fields, spreading manure, and then moved on.

Around noon, I reached a pleasant-looking village, which happened to be Stanislawow, the very same village Vieslaw's girlfriend and her father lived in. Somehow, I found the little six-morg farm, and walked into the living room, which was familiar from Vieslaw's descriptions, with its dining table. Maria and her father were at home. I introduced myself and conveyed greetings from Vieslaw. The girl, who was tall, thin, and thirtyish, blushed. Her father was sombre. Upon my solicitation of a job, he answered that he could not afford any help. He was a tenant farmer, and that was the reason he had let Vieslaw go.

I departed after this exchange, but I still liked the appearance of the farms, ranged along a wider-than-usual road. The houses were on one side, with the fields and fruit orchards on the other.

I tried to make a careful choice selecting my next employer—after all, my life could very well depend on it.

Such simple things as the condition of the paint on fences and buildings and the presence or absence of weeds in the yard were visible signs to be carefully pondered before knocking on doors. A roof in poor repair, I thought, was not a sign of poverty but rather of laziness. It does not take any money to repair a thatched roof, just willingness to work and a healthy frame of mind.

Another important factor was the size of the farm. I had learned that a very small farmer would be too poor to keep me. A very wealthy farmer would be more likely to insist on my having documents, which—since I was not able to provide any—could result in hazardous exposure, with unpredictable consequences.

I was walking by a large, newly built red-brick house. Behind it, I could see the other farm buildings—medium-sized and well cared for. The size was right. The atmosphere was right. I decided to ask for work, and walked in.

A tall man, wearing a sea captain's hat, was repairing a barn wall. With a large hammer in his hand, he was pounding nails into the boards. He was a mustached, middle-aged man with protruding cheekbones, which gave his eyes a slanted look. He stopped hammering as he saw me approaching him.

"*Dzien dobry* [good day]," I said.

"*Dzien dobry*," answered the man.

"I'm looking for work," I ventured.

"What kind of work? Cowherding?" asked the man, as he looked me over.

"Yes," I replied. The man looked at me thoughtfully for a few moments.

"Wait," he said, "I'll call my wife." He turned towards the house and called, "Mariana!" A large, red-cheeked woman wearing a wide skirt, an apron, and a kerchief on her head came out and walked towards us. She seemed about the same age as the man and must have been very pretty when she was young. In fact, they were both healthy-looking people and I thought they made a good couple.

I was standing close to the centre of the yard, which was surrounded by the usual four buildings. These, judging by their appearance, were well built and well maintained. The horse stable and toolshed were one long building, made of grey concrete blocks and covered with a black tar-paper roof. Across from this building was a cowshed, older and with a thatched roof, matching the wooden barn, but brightly whitewashed, its roof and windows intact. The red-brick house had an entrance in the centre, and a brick wood stove could be seen through the open door—large, black iron pots steaming on it. Potatoes for the pigs, I thought.

My appraisal of the surroundings was interrupted by the man's voice, speaking to his wife: "This boy wants to do our cowherding. What do you think?"

"We need a boy," she said, "and he looks all right."

"All right, then. How much do you ask a month?"

"I'll work for my clothes," I answered. I could have asked for 300 zlotys per month, but then I would have had to go to town to buy clothes. In spite of the bad experience with the Bargiels, I preferred to avoid the necessity of having to enter a larger town with the police and gendarmes everywhere.

"We'll remake your old boots for him..." said the woman, obviously pleased with my terms of the agreement.

"Yes, and you can sew a jacket for him," said the man, gratified, it seemed.

He then asked my name, and the rest of the usual questions. I told him the same story I told the Bargiels, and was hired by the couple, Mr. and Mrs. Zdziech. My name was still Joziek, Joseph Szalewski in full. When Mrs. Zdziech reached out for my basket of clothes, I told her, "There are lice in these clothes."

She took the basket anyway and, with a farmer's resourcefulness, buried it in the ground and left it there for two weeks. At the end of that period she dug it out, cooked the clothes in a large kettle for a few hours, then washed them. There were no more lice in the clothes after that. She also cut my blue winter coat apart at the seams and, after discarding the tattered and worn parts, sewed a nice, tight jacket for me. It reached a little below the waist and looked like an officer's jacket, except for the colour.

The Zdziechs had four children: three sons and a daughter. Only two of the sons were on the farm. The third, an officer in the Polish army, had been a German prisoner of war since the occupation of Poland in 1939. The daughter was married to a nearby well-to-do miller and had two daughters, aged five and seven.

One of the sons who lived on the farm, the youngest, named Stanislaw, was a handsome if not overly pretty boy of twenty-one, with rosy cheeks like his mother's. The other boy, Wladek, suffered from a malady rendering him unsuitable for marriage or any type of normal life, for that matter.

They said that when Wladek was twelve, he used to sleepwalk. One night, his father followed him, and, thinking he could cure him of his nocturnal wandering, hit him with a leather belt across his back. Wladek was never the same after that. When he walked, he stooped forward, saliva flowing out of his half-open mouth, his hands hanging down lifelessly. Every step he took looked like his last one because of his staggering walk. But he was surprisingly agile, and could run very fast if he wanted to.

In fact, I thought Wladek was more intelligent than anyone else in the family and had great kindness and compassion for people—certainly more than they had for him. He had a sense of humour and laughed often, with the uncontrollable laugh of a moron. He cried, too, when his father, carrying the guilt and shame of having an abnormal offspring, called him a cripple, an idiot. Despite this, Wladek was good-hearted and never carried a grudge.

There was also Zdziech's mother, a tiny, dried-up woman, her grey hair tied into a bun. She was over seventy years old, but still in full possession of all her faculties. She even had all of her original teeth. She had her own room in the house, did her own cleaning and washing, and milked her own cow, an old black-and-white animal with its ribs showing and a quizzical look on its face. The old lady made butter and cheese and sold them very profitably to smugglers, who took them to Warsaw by train.

Farmers who had enough land to make farming worthwhile were very prosperous because of the high food prices, even though they had to deliver a portion of their harvest to the Germans. This was called "*Kontingent*," and they even got paid for that—not at its true value, but in the form of coupons redeemable for textiles, cigarettes, general merchandise, and alcohol. They could keep the rest of the harvest, or sell it officially at unrealistically low prices set by the Germans. Very few farmers, if any, did that. Usually, they sold their surplus at black-market prices. They were actually able to expand and improve their farms and put up new buildings, if materials and permits could be obtained. Bribing the Germans and Poles in charge of these things helped.

I now had seven cows and two yearlings to take care of. The pasture was two kilometres from the farm. The land there was too poor for growing regular crops, and was parcelled out among the farmers in the area, from other villages as well as Stanislawow. The grass was sharp edged and had a pungent smell, reminiscent of some ferns. Boys and girls from several villages came every day, each with his or her own little herd, feeding on the youngster's piece of the pasture. They were good kids, quite sensible too, seldom behaving wildly, and very soon I was on friendly terms with all of them. We baked potatoes together. One brought the potatoes, another salt, and still another one, a few matches.

For fuel, we used dry manure. Occasionally, there was a piece of butter to rub on the steaming potatoes, making it a real treat. Some kids sang songs, some talked, and some liked nothing better than to lie on their backs and look up at the sky. I enjoyed all these things, but I still dreamed of having a musical instrument.

Then one day my pastoral existence was shaken, and life was never the same again. Black clouds of smoke hung over Warsaw. I heard the news as the word spread to the farmers: the Warsaw Ghetto had risen to fight its German oppressors!

The people of the Ghetto were putting up a heroic fight. Heroic and hopeless. The Germans threw everything they had against them: bombs, cannon, tanks, and hundreds of soldiers. Soon they stopped sending tanks. Too many of them were burned, destroyed by the Jewish fighters who had scant weapons and used makeshift grenades made of empty tin cans and Molotov cocktails thrown by people who gave their lives to destroy the German tanks.

Too many Germans were killed for their own comfort, the farmers were saying, so they stopped sending German troops, and used their "helpers" instead: the Latvians and Ukrainians who made the mistake of joining them, betraying their own people. The Jews fought from every house and every window—so the German "Supermen," unable to face them on even terms, resorted to bombing house after house with explosives, artillery, and fire bombs. Yet the Jews fought on, from cellars and ruins. They fought to the end.

Very few Poles offered help. They didn't help the Germans either. Most of them stood back. I listened to these news reports with pain in my heart. I masked my face and cried when I was alone. I could not forgive myself for leaving my brother there. What was he doing now? Was he alive? I was torn inside. What was I to do? Go back? I wouldn't get very far. It would be useless and foolish. Still, I might get close to the Ghetto. But what then? Wait outside and watch the massacre at close range? Or try to enter the Ghetto and die fighting alongside my compatriots?

Even if I could get back into the Ghetto, it made me sick to think of killing anyone—even a German. I was angry at myself for my inability to hate. So I did nothing. It was intolerable. I, a Jew, did nothing to help my brothers. I prayed to God to help them and watched in helpless agony, the black smoke during the days, the red skies at nights.

My family was dying there...and fighting. I could not picture them fighting. They were all such peaceful people. One Pole said, "To hell with the Jews! Who cares about them. It's a shame, though, that a big chunk of Warsaw is being destroyed." I felt sick. I almost hated the man, but then I took a good look at him, and felt sorry for him instead.

All I could think about was those once-peaceful people fighting. And how they were fighting! It took more time to occupy the small territory of the Warsaw Ghetto in that spring of 1943, and more German corpses, than to occupy the whole of Poland in the fall of 1939. And even then, when the whole of the Ghetto was in ruins, shots fired from cellars and handmade grenades thrown by Jewish fighters kept on blowing up German trucks and armoured cars.

Why did they do it? I knew now what my friends at Hashomer Hatzair had meant by "more cooperation between the Jewish people." I had no doubt that they had organized the uprising, but how could they have made the decision to send women and children to a certain death? I could not comprehend it. I knew them as fine, honest, idealistic young people. They must have had an overwhelming reason, but what?

I dared not criticize them. They were dying with pride while I was living in fear. But why the women and children? In vain, I searched for an answer. I did not understand—not at that time.

After what seemed like an eternity, the uprising ended. The smoke was gone from the sky. The brief glow of freedom had been extinguished. People stopped talking about it. For them, life went on as before.

The uprising of the Jews of the Warsaw Ghetto, which took place between April 19 and May 16, 1943, was history. It was the first uprising in occupied Europe. I found out later that just over a 1000 Jewish fighters, untrained and equipped with mostly hand pistols and little else, faced over two thousand Germans and their stooges. The Germans had tanks. The Jews had despair, pride, and courage.

For me, the acceptance of this incomprehensible reality—the horrible fact of being the only survivor of a family that once numbered over two hundred people—drove me to the edge of madness. My thoughts turned to memories of Aunt Cecil and her daughters Irene and Mirka.

Irene, the elder sister, was a chestnut-haired teenager who had a lovely singing voice. She had to wear a heavy brace on her leg, which was crippled by tuberculosis of the bone. The brace was made of leather, reinforced by steel hinges above and below her knee, with an elevated metal heel acting as support. But in spite of her handicap, she was a lively and positive person who sang popular songs all day long. Without being aware of it, I had absorbed and stored in my mind's musical memory the songs she once sang. Irene's other great passion was meticulously rolling her long auburn hair into curls like Shirley Temple's.

My younger cousin, Mirka, was about my age, blue-eyed and shy, and very quiet in contrast to her sister. When Mirowska Street was excluded from the Ghetto, our ways parted and we had to move in with Aunt Lea and her three children at 31 Gesia Street. There was not enough room for Aunt Cecil and her two daughters, and they were forced to move elsewhere.

I saw them only once after that, sometime later in the winter of 1941–42. It was at a flea market near Pawia. Aunt Cecil and Mirka were bundled up in all kinds of rag-tag angular kerchiefs and frazzled, triangular shawls, trying to squeeze out an existence by selling little bundles of kindling wood. Their hands were clad in fingerless gloves, and they were stamping their feet and flailing their arms, trying to keep from freezing in the bitter cold. They were pale, and their sunken eyes showed signs of starvation.

To this day, I don't know what became of them. Aunt Cecil explained that Irene was at home, in bed in a one-room, unheated hovel, wrapped in old blankets and duvets, waiting for something to eat. I never saw Irene again.

The Warsaw Ghetto is no more, no more, no more, echoed endlessly within my confused mind. I went though the motions of performing my daily routines without feeling anything at all. I tried to recall how I felt when Uncle Shmuel died, and shift it to the loss of my whole family so that I could cry. I tried to recall the moment I was told that my mother was taken away. It hurt, but my eyes were still dry, my feelings frozen. I held tightly to my last memory of my father, waving good-bye from the back of a truck bound for Russia in February of 1940.

I still desperately hoped that my parents were alive. My mother, beyond some unknown river where she had supposedly been resettled by the Germans. My father, somewhere in Russia. I tried not to think of my brother, my uncles, aunts, and cousins. I tried to share David's agony when his father was made to drown in his presence. I needed all my strength to recall the arguments I'd quoted to David when he had contemplated giving himself up to the Germans: "Don't give up hope! Your life is precious! Don't make a gift of it to the Germans! Be strong and patient!"

I hadn't been able to stop David from resigning himself to the false idea that others, through brute force, have the right to dispose of or use the lives of other human beings. I now had to repeat my own argument back to myself. But my belief in the ultimate victory of good over evil, my own words, were hollow and unconvincing to me now. Mere words, trying to rationalize unbearable reality.

Several days passed without change until one evening, when I heard the sound of a harmonica being played by an neighbouring farmer. My eyes swelled with uncontrollable tears. Oh, to have an instrument! To be able to express my feelings instead of just choking them off! I started walking towards the farm, but just then I heard singing. It sounded beautiful, and seemed to be coming from the west, where the reddish evening sky glowed softly. I thought that I recognized the song. Yes, it was one of the songs in the little black book I'd received from Mrs. Dahlen.

I walked faster towards the singing, and spotted the singers upon reaching the village. They were young village people, a group of seven or eight of them, standing in a semi-circle around a large wooden cross on the roadside. It was black with age, and leaned to one side. I stood and listened for a while. The song was about a little girl named Bernadette who saw Mary and talked to her. The words didn't matter to me—I am a Jew. But the melody was beautiful.

I felt an irresistible urge to sing as I came closer, and joined them. At first I participated quietly and shyly, then louder and more boldly. The song ended, then someone started another song, which I also knew, and again I sang along with the others. Then the next one, and the next one...I experienced an emotional catharsis. I could cry again, and I did, later that night when I was alone, feeling better and stronger afterwards.

I slept in the stable loft, which was half filled with soft, fragrant hay. The stable was in a long, cement-block building, covered by a black tar-paper roof, and divided into two parts by a brick wall. One part served as a horse stable, and the other side was a tool room. The stable housed three horses: two fat Belgian pull-horses, a brother and sister, marbled in two shades of beige, and a third horse, a brown mare, lame in her right hind foot but still earning her keep by pulling a plow or a cultivator. I thought that it was kind of the Zdziechs to keep a crippled horse.

The tool room served as a hiding place for five illegal piglets, illegal meaning they had not been reported to the Germans when they were born, and therefore were not wearing metal tags on their ears as registered animals did. The hayloft entrance was through the tool room; a ladder affixed to the wall lead to a trapdoor in the ceiling. There, I had my fragrant nest and a blanket provided by my employers. There was a similar trapdoor over the horse stable, but without the ladder. Through this opening I could relieve myself at night when the need arose. There was also a dormer protruding from the middle of the roof, where a door could be opened for loading hay into the loft.

Singing under the cross continued throughout the rest of the month of May. I not only took part in it, but gradually took over the leadership of the group. My voice was good, and trained with the Faiwuszyc Choir of the Warsaw

Ghetto. My clear city accent and fluent reading were assets as well. The other singers started to look to me as their choir leader.

But Mr. Zdziech had a different opinion. He thought that his cowherd ought to be asleep at this hour of the night. (The singing usually started at eight and ended at midnight.) He tried to drive home his disapproval one night by closing the tool-room door from the inside so that I could not enter the loft. I did not let it perturb me. I took a ladder out of the barn and climbed up onto the roof. There, I opened the inside hook of the loading door with my pocket knife, pushed the ladder away, closed the loading door behind me, and went to sleep. Faced with such determination on my part, Mr. Zdziech limited his objections to murmuring under his breath about "boys dragging themselves home at all hours of the night," but didn't interfere any more. May ended, and so did the singing sessions, or *majowki*, as they were called.

Other things occupied my free time now. It is a Polish village custom to send out messenger-delivered cards on various name days designated by the Catholic calendar. I delivered some cards and received five to 10 zlotys for each. After earning a total of 50 zlotys from these deliveries, I had bought a pair of two-month-old domesticated rabbits, a male and a female. I was allowed to keep them in the tool room in an old wire cage. I fed them fresh milkweed, which I gathered every morning before taking the herd to the pastures. The rabbits were nice little creatures, spotted grey on white. I hoped that they would stay healthy and have lots of young. These I planned to sell and buy a harmonica. In the meantime, I sang songs while herding the cows. I walked barefoot at all times now, even on the fields of stubble. There was a trick to it: one had to slide one's foot over the stubble before stepping down. Until I mastered the proper way of walking, I would often cut the soles of my feet.

The Zdziechs bought a pair of pants for me—black, and made of a German paper-textile. They also provided me with a shirt, open-necked and almost new. These were the clothes I wore daily. My friends in the pastures showed me how to make a *pyta,* a long whip made of leather strips and woven so that it was thick at the handle and tapered off to a single strand at the tip. The whole whip was swivel-joined to a short wooden handle with a soft but strong strap. I learned to use it with accuracy. I could hit a small stone two metres away with its tip, and used the shot-like sound it produced to keep the cows in line, seldom touching an animal—never hitting. My complexion was brown from the day-long exposure to the sun, and my body was trim and hard. I could run like a locomotive for hours without getting tired.

My employers, the Zdziechs, had a fruit orchard right across the road opposite their house. There was an abundance of fruit. First cherries, then plums, and finally apples and pears. I ate more than my share of fruit, so much in fact that my stomach protested more than once.

My female rabbit had been expecting, and the day of delivery finally arrived. I was sitting at a bench at the rear of the house eating my usual breakfast (a deep plate of mashed potatoes with small hand-rubbed noodles covered with hot milk), when I heard Wladek's voice calling from the tool room.

"Joziek, come here quick! Your female is delivering!"

I dropped the plate and ran. It was true! Three of the little ones were already born, and three more arrived while Wladek and I looked on. The female had made a little nest in a pile of hay and covered it with her own fur, which she'd pulled out with her teeth from her own belly. She nudged her wet, blind babies into the nest. The little mouths were constantly seeking her nipples and bumping into each other in the process. After I was assured that they were all right, I went around to spread the news. But the news was known already—Wladek saw to that. I was congratulated by everyone, and there were customers aplenty for the offspring. They would have to wait a few weeks until the babies were old enough to leave their mother.

So I had my brood to look after. I gathered milkweed as before, but I had to let it dry before feeding it to the rabbits. Dew-covered leaves could blow up their tummies and make them sick.

After bringing the cows from the pastures each evening, the rabbits were my first concern. It was a week later, on a Sunday, that I saw a blue-uniformed Polish policeman standing in the Zdziechs' yard, halfway between the barn and the house. My blood ran cold. I was momentarily paralysed. To camouflage my fear, or just to appear being occupied with something—anything—I pulled out a handful of grass from a patch at the side of the horse stable and took it to my rabbits. The policeman followed me into the tool room. I stood in front of the rabbits' cage, feeding the grass to them, my heart pounding. The policeman looked around the room. His eye, trained in finding "illegal" objects for which he could extract "grease" money from the farmers, immediately spotted the four piglets hidden behind an enclosure. He grunted with obvious satisfaction and scanned the tool room for more "illegalities" that he could use to blackmail the Zdziechs. His eyes rested on me.

"What's your name, boy?" he asked. His feigned disinterest did not fool me. Afraid as I was, my mind rushed through the limited options, searching for the most appropriate response. A few moments earlier my life had been relatively safe. Now, my primary instinct for self-preservation was forced to respond to a mortal threat.

"Joziek," I said—with all the indifference I could muster. The policeman looked at me fleetingly and seemed disappointed. I continued feeding my rabbits. The policeman gave the piglets one more greedy look and left the tool room. My knees felt weak and wobbly, and spots swam in front of my eyes. I sat down on an empty crate, and as I did, I caught sight of the back of the policeman's uniform. He was standing by the rear entrance of the house, talking to the Zdziechs. He was there to see what he could extract from them for keeping silent about the piglets. As long as the policeman was still on the farm, I felt uneasy. He finally left, his crooked smile even more pleased than before.

Mr. and Mrs. Zdziech accompanied him to the gate and stood there while they were saying good-bye to him with forced smiles on their faces and fear mixed with hate in their eyes. I sighed when the blue-uniformed traitor left the farm. I knew that for a split second my life had hung on a hair, or rather on one word. Had I answered the query about my name with "Joseph Szalewski" instead of "Joziek," spoken with a rural accent, he would have without doubt made further inquiries about family documents, and that could have been the end of me. As it happened, his attention shifted to the guaranteed profit in blackmailing the Zdziechs about the illegal piglets.

There was another, lesser storm brewing that threatened my good relations with my employers. They were angry with me for leading the policeman to the piglets. Why, they wanted to know, did I feed my rabbits just as the blue-uniformed bloodsucker arrived?

It was easier for me to claim ignorance of the danger—trying to pacify the Zdziechs—than to admit my own personal vulnerability, and perhaps a desire to create a diversion, on a subconscious level, by trying to keep myself busy. This upheaval was soon over, and my life was saved for the time being.

Time passed, and my young rabbits were old enough to leave their mother. I sold them to waiting customers, receiving 75 zlotys for all six of them. I used the money to buy a harmonica from a man in the village. Now, I could play any melody in a major key, but I couldn't play any minor tunes. The harmonica was not a chromatic type, and it didn't have any half notes. That was a great handicap to me, as I always liked the warmth and melancholy depth of minor melodies. As much as I enjoyed my instrument, I wished for a more versatile one.

An accordion! That would be ideal, but I knew the cost to be beyond my means, and so I didn't really dare to nourish hope of ever owning one.

Without any warning one morning, soon after the Polish policeman's visit, Mr. Zdziech called me over to the house: "Joziek! Come over here. I want to talk to you!"

I walked over, with a strange feeling that something was wrong.

Mr. Zdziech said: "Joziek, my woman is going to Blonie [the district town]. You should be registered at the town hall. Get ready. You're going with her to get registered."

I felt cold inside. My heart pounded in my chest, and my mouth was dry. Is this the end, then? Will I run again? Sleep in the fields and dodge the Germans like a hunted animal? I liked the place and the people. They liked me. I was a human being again. I had friends. What to do...what to do. I decided to take a chance—I had to take a chance. God would help me.

We sat side by side on the high seat of the Sunday carriage. Mrs. Zdziech was holding the reins. Her lips were pressed tightly together. She, too, seemed nervous. We rode in silence all the way to town. The team of horses pulled the light carriage with ease, their fat backsides shaking with the brisk trot. The carriage was painted with black lacquer and had shiny chrome naphtha lanterns on both sides like a hearse.

We entered the town, which consisted mostly of two-storey houses, some stores, and a town hall. Mrs. Zdziech parked the carriage in front of the building. I hung feed bags around the necks of the horses. Then we walked into the town hall, and approached a small window wicket.

"Yes?" inquired the clerk from behind a wooden grate. He was dressed in civilian clothes and his accent was guttural *Volks*-German.

Mrs. Zdziech nervously explained that her worker here, Joziek, wasn't registered, and came here to be registered, and he had no papers. The clerk looked at me sharply. Somehow I was not afraid. I looked the man straight in the eyes.

"And how come you haven't any papers?" he asked, his eyes narrowing. "Every person above thirteen should have a *Kennkarte*. How come you haven't got it?" he repeated.

"Well, you see, sir, I left Warsaw after the 1939 bombardment," I said, "right after my father was killed." I lowered my eyes. "My mother died before the war and after that I lived in the country, watching cows for different farmers, going from one to the other. I never knew I had to be registered. All the papers were burned in the fire. I had no documents, no one asked for any..."

I stopped, looked at the man, and waited for the answer.

The man was studying me carefully for a few moments. Suddenly, he nodded and picked up a printed form:

"Your name?"

"Joseph Szalewski."

"Place of birth?"

"Warsaw."

"Date of birth?"

A thought shot through my mind: I might as well make myself younger, so they wouldn't take me to Germany to do forced labour.

I knew that they took people from thirteen years of age on. I made myself two years younger. I wasn't big, and I could pass. I could never recall later what happened after I gave the particulars to the clerk at the wicket. My mind was a blank. I only know that Mrs. Zdziech and I were walking into a medical office, where I received some kind of an inoculation from a man in a white coat. I regained my senses long enough to answer questions about my name and age, and gave my reduced age again.

The next thing I knew, we were walking back to the carriage and Mrs. Zdziech was putting a white slip of paper into her purse—my official receipt for the police registration as Joseph Szalewski! Her large, rosy-cheeked face, framed by a flowery kerchief, looked relieved and pleased. In my hand was a blue two-page booklet stating officially that I, Joseph Szalewski, had received the required inoculations.

All at once, an uncontrollable feeling of happiness seized my mind and soul. I wanted to laugh and laugh, but I didn't.

It would look suspicious, right after getting inoculated. I readied the horses and climbed onto the driver's seat. This time, I took the reins, made a kissing sound with my lips, and the horses started to pull. I shook the reins, and they went into a trot. When we left the streets of Blonie and reached the open road, they went like the wind. I shifted my body against the movements of the carriage on the bumpy road. We left a trail of dust behind us, and the willows on both sides of the road cried—from happiness, this time.

I placed both reins between the fingers of my left hand, and reached into my side pocket with my right hand. I fingered the cardboard texture of the blue booklet. I would have liked to take it out and look at it again, but I didn't. I had to act as any Polish boy would act when doing such unpleasant things as getting registered and inoculated. By now, I was well trained in hiding my true emotions, and instinctively knew what kind of response to a given situation would look most natural.

What to me was a passport to life—a change of status from an insecure, hunted animal to a legal person—would be a bothersome formality to the people among whom I lived. I had to be one of them. Fear meant death, literally and truly, and my Jewishness could be easily proven by my being circumcised, should my behaviour arouse suspicion that I was a Jew.

The horses trotted through the open gate. We were back home.

Controlling the cows was a problem during the hot season. Flying insects called *bonki* drove the animals almost mad. Steel-jawed beetles, the *bonki* cut right into the cows' thick hides to lay their eggs under the skin. The eggs then grew into fat larvae, which in due time worked their way out from under the skin and fell to the ground, where they went through a metamorphosis, becoming next year's *bonki*. The exit of the larvae left holes in the hides, causing pain and decreasing the milk output, not to mention the value of the hides.

The sound made by the flying beetles was a vicious "gzzzzz." A cow, after hearing that ominous sound, started what we called "gzzzying"—that is, she would lift her tail straight into the air and start running as fast as her four legs would carry her, in any direction. It became quite an achievement to chase and retrieve seven cows, each running in a different direction and, what was worse, invading other farmers' fields.

I found cows to be clever creatures, contrary to general opinion. The temptation posed by the luscious, green fields adjacent to the sparse pastureland made them stage a performance worthy of Shakespeare. While pretending indifference, they would go into the "get-into-the-green" manoeuvre by edging closer and closer to the forbidden fields. Keeping their steaming, wet mouths close to the ground, they made swiping motions with their tongues, quite realistically, but without actually eating a single blade of grass. They continued this mime act while steadily progressing towards the fields. When they were very close to their goal, excitement made them drop part of their pretence. Their tongues became idle, but they still went through the motions of eating. They sniffed excitedly, their eyes turning to see if I was watching. Then, the oldest cow gave the signal by abandoning the play-acting and running into the green, usually followed by the rest of the herd.

About halfway between farm and pastureland was a small, shallow lake. During the hot season it was dried up to no more than a puddle, but one good rain could restore it to normal size. I sometimes cooled off in it on my way to the pasture by jumping in for a quick splash. Since I did not own swimming trunks, I used my underpants instead, removing them in the bushes afterwards and carrying them in my hands the rest of the way.

Autumn of 1943 arrived. I worked with Mr. Zdzeich and his sons, bringing in the potatoes and burying them in long piles, covered by layers of earth and straw. The previously harvested grain crops were stored inside the barn, tied into countless little bundles that reached all the way up to the roof beams. After the potatoes were safely buried in their winterized mounds, it was time to thrash the grain.

A red gasoline-driven thrashing machine was rented. The bundles were thrown one at a time into the revolving mouth of the machine, and the precious grain was extracted. All this was accompanied by a terrific clatter and clouds of dust. I was stationed on top of the barn, throwing the bundles to Mr. Zdziech, who fed them into the thrasher. Stanislaw heaved and carried out grain-filled burlap bags at the rear, while Wladek pitchforked the straw to the side of the building.

Days pass quickly at harvest time and in the weeks following the harvest, when preparations are made for the coming winter. After working hard from early morning until late at night, six days a week, I appreciated a day of rest so much more. On Sundays, I spent my time visiting neighbours, playing my harmonica, and resting.

The weather was still mild, and on days when my help was not needed at home, I took the cows out to pasture. One day after returning with the cows, I was told by Wladek that there was a piano in the living room. It belonged to the Zdziechs' daughter, Mrs. Michalowska. She had bought it for her daughters and was keeping it at her parents' home for a while owing to lack of space in her own house.

I had never set foot in the living room of the house. I didn't even know what it looked like. There was an unwritten law: a hired hand's bare feet weren't supposed to walk on his employer's living-room floor, not at the Bargiels' place and not here. A farmer's living room—even if the house only had two rooms and was used as a bedroom—was his private sanctuary, setting the distinction between him and his worker (who was not a member of the family).

Still, the piano was there, and I couldn't rest knowing of its presence and longing to play it. The following day was Sunday. Shortly after breakfast, Mrs. Michalowska's carriage appeared in front of the gate. Her two girls were with her, and they came to see the new piano and to visit their grandparents. I opened the gate and helped tie up the horses. As I did that, I told Mrs. Michalowska that my mother had taught me to play the piano when I was little. Mrs. Michalowska was genuinely surprised.

She never would have imagined, she said. Would I come into the living room and try out her piano?

"Oh, yes, but are you sure it's all right?" I asked hesitantly.

"Certainly!" replied Mrs. Michalowska. "How else are we going to find out if the piano arrived undamaged over the rough journey from the city?" No one else knew how to play the piano. With that assurance and support behind me, I followed Mrs. Michalowska and the girls into the house and into the living room.

There it was. A small, light brown, upright piano with a bench standing invitingly in front of it. I approached it— my heart beating—sat down, and opened the top slowly, almost reverently. I tried a chord, then a scale, then an arpeggio. Then I played a song my mother had taught me and tears flooded my eyes, rolled down my cheeks, and fell on my dusty pants. I continued playing, oblivious of my surroundings. One song followed another, like a cloudburst after a long drought. I poured out all that was in my heart. For the moment, I was home with my parents, and my brother, surrounded by their love.

I was brought back to reality by the sound of Mrs. Michalowska's voice. Oh, she said, I played so beautifully! Could I teach Zosia? she asked.

Zosia was her elder, eight-year-old daughter. Here was a chance to have access to the instrument more often. I agreed, provided that Mrs. Michalowska supply me with a book titled *Rozycki's Music School for Piano, Opus 1*. My mother used this very book when she began to teach me. Mrs. Michalowska promised she would drive to Blonie first thing the next morning and get the book.

Every Sunday for the next five months, I gave Zosia a one-hour piano lesson. At the end of that time, she could read notes with a good degree of fluency, and played little pieces out of the book with both hands, to the proud satisfaction of her mother, grandmother, and great-grandmother. Mr. Zdziech was against it from the beginning. Not openly because, after all, it was his daughter's piano standing in the living room and he dared not oppose the lessons. But I could hear him muttering under his mustache things like: "What is the world coming to, when barefoot cowhands march right into the living room as if they own it."

I could not help being barefoot. I simply didn't have any shoes. My old shoes had gone to pieces a long time ago, and the Zdziechs still hadn't given the old boots to a shoemaker to be rebuilt for me, as they'd promised to do when they hired me. I kept on reassuring myself with rationalizations, such as, They are waiting for the cold weather to come, or, Who needs shoes in the summer?—except in the living room, that is. Finally, in November, they took the boots to the village shoemaker. But instead of remaking them into boots for me, he converted them into ladies' boots—on Mrs. Zdziech's orders—for her own use. My shoes, when I finally got them by the end of November, turned out to be a pair of low, laced remakes of Wladek's old shoes.

I was deeply hurt by the broken promise, perhaps because I had genuine affection and respect for my employers and deemed them to be trustworthy and honest. My incognito existence notwithstanding, high leather boots were the dream of every boy in the Polish countryside. Thus, my naive faith in the few people I thought I could trust had been shaken, and there was little I could do about it. Besides, low leather shoes were better than no shoes at all.

The preparations for the Christmas holiday had started. The next-door neighbour's son, Tadeusz, was a professional butcher. He came early in the morning and slaughtered one of the illegal pigs. He then spent the rest of the day making kielbasa, smoking the bacon, and converting the leftover parts of the pig into oval headcheese, called *salceson*. Caution had to be used when smoking meats such as ham and bacon—the smell could attract all kinds of blackmailers, especially the Polish police. The finished products were hung from the rafters of the loft, under the roof of the house. The Zdziechs also bought a whole galvanized milk can of moonshine vodka and left it standing in the anteroom, just off the little room where Wladek and Stanislaw slept.

The following Sunday afternoon, the Zdziech family, with the exception of Wladek, rode away in the black carriage to visit their friends and relatives in another village. The weather was cold. Wladek and I stayed at the house and played checkers, a game I had constructed out of wooden disks and a half-filled bottle of black ink that I'd discovered in the tool room. I taught Wladek the rules, and he played quite well, winning at least half of our games.

That afternoon, however, he played poorly and finally gave up. He suddenly rose. His face broke into a wide grin and he laughed mischievously. He went into the kitchen and came back with a long-handled half-litre measuring cup for milk. He carried two tea glasses in his other hand and he giggled, amused by his own resourcefulness. He opened the lid of the shiny, galvanized milk can and dipped the tin cup into the brew. The nod of his chin told me that he was asking me to hold the glasses for him. I complied, and Wladek filled the glasses almost to the brim.

"Take it," he said, picking up one of the glasses. We clinked our glasses and emptied them in one continuous motion. The homemade vodka was sweet and palatable. We clinked our glasses several more times as I poured the potent brew down my throat. Wladek didn't water any flowers with his glassful either. By the time the rest of the family returned home, the two of us were in the best of spirits, singing and laughing at anything at all. The Zdziechs were so taken by the scene that they were not angry with us. Instead, they laughed at our antics until they couldn't laugh any more. And I had my first hangover the following morning.

January 1944 was here. My sleeping place in the tool-room loft became too cold, and I was permitted to sleep in the house, sharing Wladek's bed. For reasons I could not imagine, Mrs. Zdziech hung her bulky underwear on Wladek's bedpost on the way to her bedroom. The traditional bloomers have a centre slit for a practical reason— namely, so that a woman could urinate while working in the fields without having to squat down. All she had to do was spread her legs and keep her wide skirt out of the way. It saved time, and besides, the cows and the mares did it all the time. It was natural. What was unnatural was Mrs. Zdziech's habit of hanging the perceptibly odoriferous and visibly moist garment on her incapacitated son's bedpost every night.

Some light was thrown on the mystery of the bloomers when Mrs. Zdziech, somewhat abashedly, related to me that they had tried to provide Wladek with the services of a prostitute sometime earlier. "Without success, needless to say," sighed Mrs. Zdziech. With saliva flowing out of his half-open mouth and his idiot's laughter, not even a professional prostitute could be persuaded to offer her services, which, they had been told by a reliable authority, could cure Wladek of his malady. Motivated no doubt by guilty feelings about Wladek's condition—her husband had hit him while he was sleepwalking—she ended her unexpected explanation with an unspoken, unclear plea. It sounded like an appeal for me to somehow help to "relieve" the situation.

I was shocked. So she put the smelly bloomers on the bedpost in hopes of arousing her son's sexual appetites, which, she hoped, would translate into yearnings for me!

What nonsense. I realized that the Zdziechs and the Bargiels had more in common than I had thought in their dealings with servants. This seems to be a common thread throughout human history. People using people unscrupulously when force puts power into their hands. I resolved to maintain my principles. I also decided to try to keep my own power—small as it might be—at maximum, while trying to keep my adversary's power over me at minimum.

The first step in that direction was my immediate return to my sleeping quarters over the tool room. I survived the bitter February cold by shaping a nest in the hay and wrapping two heavy horse blankets around myself. The Zdziechs did not question my move, and since during winter months there was less work to be done, I often stayed in the house reading a book of Polish songs and poems. Some pages were missing and some torn, but it was a thick volume, a treasury of beautiful thoughts. I read it over a dozen times during the long winter evenings.

Sometimes, immersed in the pages of the book, I recalled scenes of the Warsaw Ghetto. I closed my eyes and saw myself pushing a baby carriage with Jerzyk in it. It was the corner of Elektoralna and Solna in the fall of 1940. This was always a crowded corner, but this time I could hardly make my way through it. A group of young punks around me, I somehow managed to push the baby carriage through the maze of arms and legs. When I reached an uncrowded space, I discovered that my new wallet had vanished from my jacket pocket. Proud of my earnings from candy smuggling, I'd recently bought a stiff new wallet—easy game for the resourceful pickpockets, especially since my hands were both firmly fastened to the baby carriage handles. When I got home, I threw myself on my bed and cried. My thoughts now turned to Jerzyk... What had happened to my brother, I wondered. Where was he now?

These painful thoughts were interrupted by a loud noise. The door flew open, and a man wearing a black cloth over his face and holding a handgun walked in. There were other men with covered faces and guns in their hands behind him. "Everyone face the wall, with your hands up!" he shouted in Polish.

Everyone complied. This man then stood there with his gun pointed at our backs, while the other men, four or five of them, ran through the house picking things up and carrying them outside. The whole thing took only a few minutes. As they left, the man who pointed the gun warned everyone not to leave the house for fifteen minutes. He cautioned that one of them would remain behind, watching the house, and he would shoot anyone who tried to open the door. There was no telephone service in the village. The Zdziechs waited a full half-hour before opening the door and looking out, for who could be sure that the robbers weren't bluffing? The Zdziechs did not take the incident as seriously as might have been expected. I had the impression that they were relieved that the large bundle of money they had hidden in a hole in the floor had not been discovered by the thieves.

March signals the beginning of spring in Poland. There are rare years when it snows even in May, but mostly the sun is warm, causing the snow and ice to melt quickly. Soon the cows are taken out to green pasture, and another season begins.

The agreement I had made with the Zdziechs almost a year earlier to be paid in clothing was bad business. They had bought me one pair of pants and retreaded my old jacket. They also gave me two old shirts and Wladek's shoes instead of the high boots they had promised. This was my full pay for a year's work. I had neither socks nor underwear, and my only pair of pants were giving way in places.

After the Easter holidays, which marked the anniversary of our agreement, I spoke to Mr. Zdziech. I told him that I wanted a new agreement. I asked to be paid by the month—300 zlotys per month from then on. Zdziech had a talk with his wife and came back with their answer—they had accepted my demands. Now, I could look forward to the end of each month, when I could go to Blonie and buy my own clothes.

Mother Nature had started a new cycle. The air was filled with the fragrant breath of the pregnant earth. Random breezes seemed to rock the warm rays of the sun, and the migratory birds back from the south were busily building their summer homes. I was out again in the pastures with my small herd. The old cow belonging to Mr. Zdziech's mother had died during the winter. In its place, she was given a black two-year-old. The herd had not decreased, however, because two calves were born in the meantime. They tagged along with the rest, bringing the number of animals to an even ten.

The piano lessons I was giving to Zosia had ended. Her parents had built an addition of two extra rooms onto their house. The piano was moved into one of these rooms. I informed Mrs. Michalowska that I had taught her daughter everything I could. She needed a more advanced teacher now. Mrs. Michalowska thanked me warmly for teaching her daughter so well. She read music fluently and played all the pieces in the book except the last ones, which were arranged for more advanced students.

Mrs. Michalowska asked me how she could repay me for my work. I had heard from Zosia that there was a violin at her house. No one there knew how to play it. It was just lying in the cupboard, unused. I asked if I could borrow the violin for a while.

"But of course!" said Mrs. Michalowska. "Come along with me now," she suggested, "and you can have it right away!"

I was overjoyed! I jumped onto the carriage. The miller's house was only two kilometres away from the Zdziech farm, but it seemed more like ten. I walked back, carrying the precious instrument under my arm since there was no case for it. Herding the cows was a lot more fun now. I learned how to tune the four strings and how to use my fingers. The rest was a matter of practice. By the end of April, I could play more than a hundred songs. Mostly Polish folk songs and popular tunes, but also the classics and semi-classics my mother used to play on her piano. I grew up hearing the melodies from when I was still in the cradle, and maybe even before I was born.

But the voice of a violin, no matter how beautiful, how pure or soulful, is only a thin, single voice. I loved to play the violin, but still wished I had an accordion. That was an instrument with which I could not only play the melody but accompany myself as well, giving the background, setting the mood, the rhythm, the harmony. What's more, an accordion is portable enough to carry wherever I went. The other youngsters herding their cows in the pastures liked listening to my violin. Now and then, a boy or girl asked me to play a favourite song. I always complied with their various requests. I appreciated being liked, and I enjoyed pleasing others.

May arrived, and the singers gathered once again under the wooden cross. I joined them for a while, but about halfway through the month my voice began to change, and I had to stop singing altogether.

I sold my two rabbits and kept a couple of young females. Keeping males was unprofitable. One could always take a female to a male to be impregnated.

My second payday since the start of my new agreement had arrived. I had saved my first pay, plus the proceeds from the sale of my rabbits, including three babies (one died at birth). I was getting ready to go to Blonie to buy a new pair of pants. Mrs. Zdziech allowed me to wear her boots for the occasion. The boots had ladies' half-heels and they pinched, but one had to look decent in town. I walked the eight kilometres to Blonie, and took off the boots after the first two. I carried them right up to the edge of town and then put them on again. I went to the open market and picked out a pair of pants, a shirt, a pair of socks, and underpants. That took all my money.

I walked to the edge of town wearing the boots, then took them off and never again subjected my feet to the torture of wearing those boots. In spite of the discomfort, it felt good to buy my own clothes with my own money. No one bothered me while I was in town. Some people looked at my ladies' boots and smiled, but otherwise I hadn't attracted any undue attention.

Summer was approaching, and the weather was warm. One day, on my way back from the pastures, I stopped at the lake and jumped in for a quick splash. I got out very quickly because my herd was beginning to disperse. I rounded up the cows and went over to a sparse bush, where I took off my wet underpants.

While I stood naked, on one foot trying to put on my pants, I noticed that I was being watched. The village shoemaker's son was sitting across the small lake. It seemed to me that he was watching me intensely. My heart started to pound. I thought, He saw that I'm circumcised! He knows I'm a Jew!

I dressed quickly, rounded up the cows, and rushed

them home as fast as I could. I felt uneasy that night and the following morning. I took the herd to the pastures. When I got there, I sat down and worried about my predicament without arriving at any solution to my problem.

A boy approached me and started a friendly conversation. His trimmed light hair framed a pleasant blue-eyed face, and his behaviour was exquisitely delicate in using hand gestures as he spoke. His name, he said, was Bronislaw Hylek, Bronek for short. He was my age and was studying to become a priest. His father did not want him to work on their farm. Today was an exception, since his older brother and sister were working in the fields, and their cowherd had left them a few days earlier. They were looking for a new boy, but so far could not find one.

My mind was troubled, and I was not paying full attention to Bronek's talk, until the last sentence sank in: they were looking for a new boy...

That's one way out, I thought—move to another village and hope that the shoemaker's son will soon forget what he saw—if he saw it, and if he even knew what it meant. But I could not take the chance of being recognized again.

"Where is your family this morning?"

"Over there," replied Bronek, pointing. "The first field at the end of the pastures." It wasn't far away.

"Would you watch my cows for me while I talk to your father?" I asked, and added, "I may have a boy for him."

"Sure," agreed Bronek, "but don't be long."

"I won't," I said and started to run in the direction

Bronek had indicated.

I reached the end of the pastures, where some farmers who owned less property had plowed under some of the sour grass at the edge of the pastures. They tried to raise regular crops, mostly potatoes and sugar beets. I saw a group of four people weeding a field of sugar beets. The weeds grew in profusion, more so than the sugar beets. I walked over to a thin, mustached man who worked with a younger man beside him. Two women worked on the other side of the field. All four lifted their heads and looked at me as I stopped in front of the older man.

"*Dzien dobry,*" I greeted him.

"*Dzien dobry,*" answered the man, with a weak smile. His face was weather-worn and his mustache looked as if some parts of it were missing. His face had a few days' stubble, making him look older from afar. He was about forty-five, but looked fifty-five.

The younger man with him was the same build and height, minus the mustache and stubble. He looked about twenty-two years old. Another thing they had in common was the expression in their grey, deeply set eyes. It was distrust and dissatisfaction, the latter more pronounced in the older man.

"Are you Mr. Hylek?"

"I am," answered the man. He seemed surprised that I knew his name.

"I was told you're looking for a cowherd," I ventured cautiously.

"That's true," the man confirmed with a nod. "Who told you?"

"Your son, Bronek," I waited for Mr. Hylek to speak.

"Where do you stay now?" asked Mr. Hylek.

"In Stanislawow," I told him, "and I'm tired of walking the cows from the pasture every day."

"Who do you work for?"

"Jan Zdziech."

"Don't know him," said Mr. Hylek, and asked, "What does he pay you?"

"Three hundred zlotys a month."

Mr. Hylek studied me for a few moments. "I'll pay you the same," he said.

I was glad. "Good," I said. "When do you want me to start?"

"As soon as you can come."

"Tomorrow?" Mr. Hylek seemed to be pleasantly surprised.

"Tomorrow morning, if you want," he said.

"Good," I said sombrely. "I will be at your place tomorrow morning."

"Do you know how to get there?" asked Mr. Hylek, assuming the tone of voice of an employer.

"Bronek will tell me," I said. "I have to go back now. *Dowidzenia* [till we meet again]."

"*Dowidzenia*," replied Mr. Hylek. "Tomorrow morning."

"Yes, tomorrow morning," I repeated, and started to walk back towards the pastures.

"Hey!" called Mr. Hylek after me. "What's your name?"

"Joziek, Joseph Szalewski." As I turned to face him, he acknowledged that he had heard me by nodding and I turned and started to run back to Bronek. Back with the herd, I shared the good news with Bronek. He laughed, glad that he wouldn't have to herd cows any more, and also because he liked me—he told me—and he knew that we would be good friends.

I woke up around five o'clock in the morning the next day, knowing that there was something I had to do. Oh yes, this was the day I was leaving the Zdziechs. I had an appointment with Mr. Hylek, my new employer. I dressed quickly, picked up a few of my things and climbed down the ladder into the tool room below. I packed my belongings into two bundles, one for each hand.

I worked in the semi-darkness. Only a little greyness seeping through a crack between the door and its frame made the outlines of objects visible to my wide-open eyes. I held the torn, coverless book of poetry in my hands, undecided. It did not belong to me, but then, who else used it? It was not like stealing, I convinced myself—if I leave it behind, no one will look at it. And all this treasure of written language was a window to truth and beauty. I packed it with the rest of my things. That still left my two rabbits and Mrs. Michalowska's violin. After a moment's reflection, I took my old black pants out of a bundle. I tied each cuff-end into a knot, took the rabbits from their cage one at a time, and placed the struggling animals one in each pant leg. That accomplished, I hung the pants around my neck so that the rabbits were in front, on my chest. They were moving frantically inside the pant legs, but the assembly was secure. Now, the violin. I tied the bow to the neck of the instrument and stuck it under my arm. Then I opened the door quietly.

I went back and picked up the bundles with either hand. The rabbits were hanging around my neck. The violin was under my arm. I was ready to go. My bare feet made almost no sound as I tiptoed towards the back gate, near the barn. The gate squeaked a little as it opened. I stopped and listened. All was quiet and dark in the red-brick house.

I walked out.

# part three

—

As I walked on the narrow strip of no-man's land dividing Jan Zdziech's property from that of his neighbours, I could feel the cuffs of my pants, damp with the morning dew, against my bare ankles. The wheat fields on both sides were moving in soft waves in the morning breeze. Daybreak grey skies began giving way to the rosy halo of the rising sun. I walked briskly.

I held the bundles containing my few possessions high above the wet grain, which made it difficult to keep the violin from sliding out from under my arm. The two baby rabbits, tied into the legs of my black pants and slung around my neck, were resting quietly now. I felt the warmth of their bodies and their quick heartbeats against my chest.

At the far side of the fields, the going got easier. I could let my arms down. Soon, I arrived at a dusty village road, and I followed it, my bare feet picking up moist crusts of mud with each step. The sound of roosters crowing announced the coming day.

I was approaching the village of Godzice, my destination. On the left side I saw a large estate surrounded by a barbed-wire fence. I passed a small shack-like store, standing alone at the intersection of two sandy roads. The village proper was just ahead. Most of its whitewashed mud-brick houses were on the right side of the road. Each farmer had fields stretching behind his farm buildings, as well as across the road. The sun was half out now, and there was smoke rising from some of the brick chimneys. A dog was barking behind one of the whitewashed fences.

I counted the farmhouses as I passed them. Bronek had told me that theirs was the seventh house coming from that direction. He also described the house as standing sideways to the road, with a whitewashed fence and a wooden bench in front of it. I saw it now. Five, six, seven. Yes, this was the one.

I lifted the hook on the gate and walked into the yard. A mongrel, tied to a doghouse, started to pull on his chain, barking loudly. The door opened and an aproned woman in her early forties came out and looked me over with suspicion. Though she might have been pretty once, now she had the dried-up look of someone who lives a puritanical life and doesn't enjoy it.

"*Dzien dobry*. I am Joziek, your new cowherd," I reassured her. The woman's face brightened a bit.

"You're early," she said, and motioned to the door. I

noticed that her hand was covered with flour. Making noodles, I thought, and suddenly I was hungry. The woman was wearing a long grey dress, full sleeved and closed high at the neck. Her dark brown, greying hair was tied into a bun, and she had prominent cheekbones. Her grey eyes tried to smile at me and her narrow, pale lips were aiding in the effort, revealing white, widely spaced teeth.

I had to enter the door sideways, because of the bundles in my hands and the violin under my arm. I walked into a whitewashed kitchen, half of which was dominated by an earthen cooking stove. Two black cauldrons filled with potatoes were steaming on the stove, one holding peeled ones and the other, brown-skinned spuds.

To the left of me was a closed door leading, I assumed, to the "private" living room/bedroom, since the house seemed to have only three rooms. To the right was an open door, which led to a combined dining room/bedroom. There, against a wall, stood an iron-frame bed occupied by two people who seemed to be asleep. A wooden table under a small window, three chairs, and a four-drawer chest completed the furnishings. The place was very clean. The floor was so well scrubbed that the boards, many years old and unwaxed, shone brightly.

I put down my bundles with a sigh of relief. My hands felt stiff. Then I reached for the violin under my arm and carefully placed it on the table. I didn't quite know what to do about the rabbits. They began to feel heavy, hanging in the old pants around my neck. I turned to the woman and said, "I have a couple of rabbits. Where can I put them?"

She looked at me, gazed at my bundles, and looked up at me again, as if suspecting that I was out of my mind. "Rabbits?" she asked. "What rabbits?"

I carefully lifted the black pants from around my neck. Reaching into one pant leg, I lifted out a rabbit and held her in front of me by the scruff of the neck.

The woman laughed heartily. "So that's where you got 'em!" she chuckled. "Come," she said earnestly, "there's an empty cage in the toolshed." I followed her to a small open shed filled with farm implements and assorted junk. There, in the corner, was a chicken-wire cage with a wooden frame. I placed the animals in the cage and stood up, holding the damp and smelly pants in my hands.

"Give them to me. I'll wash them," said the woman, "and come to the house. Breakfast will be ready soon."

As I walked back into the house, I saw that the unmade bed was empty, and Bronek and the young man I saw with Mr. Hylek in the pastures the previous day were washing their faces in a basin set on the table.

"*Dzien dobry,*" I said.

"*Dzien dobry,*" answered the two.

"You're up early," said Bronek, drying his hands and face.

"I had to leave early," I answered, making room for the woman to go by as she picked up the washbasin and carried it out.

"This is my brother, Wojtek," said Bronek, pointing to the tall, thin young man.

"It's nice to know you."

Wojtek's reply was not clear, as he was drying his face with a towel as he spoke. He didn't look half as intelligent as his younger brother. Apparently, Bronek received all the education while Wojtek was being groomed to run the farm.

The bedroom door opened. Wearing suspenders over a collarless shirt, Mr. Hylek walked into the kitchen. Seeing me, he said approvingly, "You're on time, Joziek. After we eat, you can take the cows out to pasture."

"Good," I replied. The transition to my new place was easier than I had anticipated. I was given a bowl of mashed potatoes with noodles and milk, which I ate balancing the bowl on my knees, sitting, as was customary for hired hands, in front of the house.

Wojtek untied the cows in the shed and they walked out into the yard one at a time. Hylek had only four cows and a yearling, all spotted black and white. The oldest cow had a broken horn. I knew which section of the pasture belonged to Hylek, and I herded them there, holding the violin and bow under my left arm and the *pyta* in my right. I practised snapping the long, tapered leather whip in the air to produce the loudest snap without touching any of the animals. By the time I reached Hylek's pasture, the dew had evaporated in the warm sun.

I sat down and reflected on the changes that had taken place in my life. I was worried about two things: What will Jan Zdziech do when he discovers that I "resigned"? And, second worry, what will the shoemaker's son do with the knowledge that I'm a Jew? That is, if he knows I'm a Jew. So deeply was I absorbed in my thoughts that I did not notice the approach of a man driving a small herd of cows in front of him, until he was close to me. It was Stanislaw Zdziech.

The moment he saw me, he started yelling. "What are you doing here, Joziek!?" he shouted angrily.

"I work here," I replied curtly, trying to keep calm.

"You wait and see! My father will get the police after you!" he threatened. He was obviously frustrated by having to take care of the cows.

"Why?"

Stanislaw tried to think of something to say. His eyes found the violin. "You took the violin...and the book!"

"The violin was lent to me by Mrs. Michalowska. And the book, why, it's all torn. Do you need it?"

"Yes," answered Stanislaw spitefully. "I want to read it!"

"Well, in that case, I'll give it to Mrs. Michalowska when I return her violin," I replied, with as much self-assurance as I could muster. Stanislaw couldn't think of anything else to say, so he hit one of the cows with a stick, and they all leaped forward.

He followed after them, giving me a dirty look as he went by. I was not worried any more. I was fairly certain that Jan Zdziech would not report me or my escape to the police. I knew the man that much. As for the violin and the poetry book, I had no choice. Right was on their side. I decided to take both to Mrs. Michalowska's house after work. In the meantime, I played as I had never played before: "*O Moj Rozmarynie*," "*Rozkwitaly Peki Bialych* Roz," "*Goralu, Czy Ci Nie Zal*," and other Polish folk songs.

At sundown, I took the cows back home and tied them up in the stable with Bronek's help. Then I went over to the house. Mr. Hylek was sitting in the front room, at the table, making a cigarette. He crumbled some yellow home-grown tobacco leaves onto a cigarette paper, rolled it, and stuck it between his lips.

"Well, Joziek, how do you like it here?" he asked, as he stoked the wheel of a large lighter and lit the cigarette.

"Very well, Mr. Hylek," I replied. "I would like to take a walk to another town now," I added, and to answer Hylek's questioning look, I explained: "I had a talk with Zdziech's son today in the pastures. They're angry at me for leaving. And this violin"—I pointed to the instrument in my hand—"it was loaned to me by one of their relatives. They want me to return it."

"You better do it, then," decreed Mr. Hylek with appropriate severity. "How long will it take you?"

"Only an hour or so," I assured him.

"Good. Did my woman show you your sleeping place?"

"No."

"Come with me, then," said Mr. Hylek as he got up and walked to the door. He showed me a wooden bunkbed set on four round poles in the cowshed. It was under a small window. I liked that. A straw-packed burlap sack served as a mattress, and there was a grey cotton blanket. This was far better than my sleeping place at the Bargiels', where I had slept directly on straw-covered dung.

I left right after that, taking the book and the violin with me. The sun was going down, and I walked briskly. When I arrived at the miller's house, I knocked, and Mrs. Michalowska opened the door. "Joziek! What are you doing here?" she exclaimed, clearly unaware of my departure from her father's farm.

"I came to return your violin. And please, return this book to Mr. Zdziech. I don't work for him any more. I have a new place in Godzice."

"But you can still keep the violin. No one here needs it right now," said Mrs. Michalowska generously.

"No, thank you very much, but it's better that I return it now," I said, and departed quickly.

I walked back to Godzice and went into the cowshed. It had been a long day, and I was tired. I lay down on my bunk. Suddenly, I remembered that I hadn't fed the rabbits! I jumped off the bunk and went over to the toolshed. The dog knew me by now and wagged his tail. I could see the cage in the light of the full moon. The rabbits were nibbling at some salad leaves. Thank God. Someone had fed them.

I went back to my bunk and rolled onto my back. I could see the moon, large and bright, shining through the two small windowpanes. My lips started to recite a prayer. I uttered the words that came into my mind: "Great God, King of the Universe, I thank Thee for all Thou hast done for me today, and all the previous days. I thank Thee also for the kindness Thou hast placed in the hearts of Thy children, the people with whom I live." Then I faced the wall and instantly fell asleep.

Waking the next morning to the sound of milk squirting into a metal pail, I looked out from under the blanket to see Mrs. Hylek doing the milking. I waited until she finished, put aside her three-legged stool, and left carrying two half-filled pails. I jumped off my bunk and got dressed. I used the rock-weighted wooden crane at the well to pull up a bucket of water. After washing my hands and face, I ate breakfast sitting at the bench in front of the house. Then I herded the cows out to the pasture. I took my old harmonica with me. It was not a very good substitute for the violin, but it would have to do.

While the herd was grazing, my thoughts drifted to a disturbing story told by one Polish farmer to another. It went like this: A farmer spotted his neighbour burying what he thought were the remains of an illegally slaughtered pig late at night. Since he hated the man, he reported him to the German gendarmes. Upon arrival, the gendarmes made the farmer dig out the remains. As it turned out, the remains were those of a Jew murdered by the farmer. Whereupon the farmer was commended for the killing of a Jew, and the informer was severely reprimanded for making a false accusation.

Bronek arrived at noon, bringing my lunch in a double pot. It tasted good. While I ate, Bronek made me a tempting offer to buy my rabbits from me. I agreed to sell them for

60 zlotys, and we closed the deal after I brought the cows back home at night. The following day, one of the rabbits died after eating wet leaves, and Mrs. Hylek was angry with Bronek for buying the rabbits from me.

Sunday morning, the Hyleks went to church in a nearby village and took me along. This was a special occasion as Bronek was serving at the altar that day. I liked the service. I was thinking how much similarity there was between the church and a synagogue. Basically it was the same thing— people praying to God. I listened to what was spoken between Bronek and the priest.

"*Dominus vobiscum,*" intoned the priest.

"*Et cum spirito tuo,*" answered Bronek.

It was all very serious and dignified. Then the organ played and everyone sang. I sang along, my voice much improved, having changed from soprano to tenor. After the service, we walked around the small village for a while, and went home as we had come, by foot.

I knew some Latin, and when Bronek suggested that we study together, I gladly agreed. During the weeks that followed, the grazing cows looked on blandly with their almond eyes and flicked their ears, hearing the strange sounds I was making: "*Gaudeo, gaudes, gaudet, gaudemus, gaudetis, gaudent.*"

Along the country road that led to the pastures, on a corner lot, lived a poor farmer who supplemented his meagre income from farming with other occupations. He owned less than a hectare of land, not enough to keep his wife and two children supplied with food. He repaired farm machinery. He also operated a press that extracted oil from poppy seeds. And he played at weddings and parties on his chromatic accordion with its button-shaped keys. The farmer's name was Wieslaw Glina. He was about forty years old, a dark blond, blue-eyed man of heavy build and medium height. Mr. Glina's lungs had been damaged during the year he had spent in a German labour camp digging ditches. His face was always bloated, and he coughed all day. He also drank and was subject to fits of bitterness and anger. I heard about him from a boy at the pastures, and went to see him, intrigued by the fact that he was an accordion player, someone who owned and played the instrument of my dreams.

I walked across fields to his place on a Sunday afternoon. The house was small—one room and a kitchen for a family of four. The floor was made of hard earth. The man sat on a low stool under a small window. He was repairing a horse's harness, using a sharp pick and a thick, bent needle. His wife opened the door. She was slight, dark haired, and wore a black dress with large red roses printed on it. She smiled weakly as she motioned for me to come in. I greeted them, and stood at the entrance. "Come in, come in. Aren't you Hylek's cowherd? I saw you passing by with his cows."

"Yes," I replied, "I work for him."

"You carried a violin. Do you play it?" asked Glina, putting the harness down on the earthen floor.

"A little," I said. "I like accordion music much better than violin. I was told that you play the accordion."

The man's face brightened. "I play it, but it's too bad you don't like the violin. I could sell you one." I was interested, and he must have noticed. "It's come unglued on one side, but you could fix it yourself. I can show you how. Do you want to see it?"

"Yes, I'd like to see it."

He lifted his right arm as if reaching for something. "Magda!" hollered the man to his wife, who was in the kitchen. "Bring the violin!" The woman walked wordlessly into the room, opened a dark wardrobe, and brought out a violin. She put it into her husband's outstretched hand and went back into the kitchen.

"Come here," said Glina, motioning. "Look, it's not broken, only unglued." I examined the instrument and agreed with him. It was an old instrument, dark brown at the front, light brown at the back. It had many scratches, and part of the base was separated from the side, but there were no cracks in the wood.

"How much do you ask for it?" I inquired. "Just the way it is."

"Five hundred zlotys. And I'll show you how to fix it."

I had 60 zlotys from selling the rabbits. "I will give you 360."

Glina thought it over, rubbing his face. "Take it," he said.

I told him that I would give him 60 zlotys now, and the

balance at the end of the month. Glina looked disappointed, then he placed the violin in my hands and said, "You'll pay me the rest when you get paid. Give me the 60 zlotys, and you've got yourself a violin."

I paid, but wasn't through yet. "How many years have you played the accordion?" I asked. Glina smiled a sad smile. "I was the best accordion player in these parts, since I was eighteen. But now..."

He had a bad coughing spell and spat on the floor when it was over, like someone spitting out his anger. His complexion was yellowish, and there were deep circles under his eyes. "Come again. What is your name?"

"Joseph Szalewski."

"Come again, Joziek. Maybe I will feel like playing and show you my accordion. Now, here's how to fix the violin."

On the way home with my violin, clutching it tightly to my breast, I felt a sadness. I held back tears and kept on swallowing to ease the lump in my throat. I felt compassion for Mr. Glina and happiness at having my own violin, both at the same time.

At home, I glued the violin with carpenter's glue and clamped it in a press to dry as Mr. Glina had told me to do. It was solid the next day, and I took it along to the pastures. I played all day until it was time to take the cattle home.

There was red sky over Warsaw that night, just as it had been during the uprising of the Warsaw Ghetto. But this time it was the Polish uprising. It started on August 1, 1944.

Hylek's cousins came over that night from a neighbouring farm and talked about the Russians, who were just across the Vistula River. If they would only attack the Germans now, the city of Warsaw would be free! Freed by Poles! But the Russians didn't attack the next day, not the next week, or the following week.

Warsaw burned, for the third time in my memory. There was talk of English airplanes dropping supplies. Rumours circulated among the villagers. The leader of the uprising was a Polish general, Bor-Komorowski. Poles were winning, it was said. But in the end, the uprising failed.

The first signs were the evacuees—families from Warsaw assigned lodgings among the farmers. Shaken and broken up, they were among the lucky ones. Many others were sent to German labour camps. After a while, life went on as before, still under the German occupation.

Hylek's daughter, a girl of nineteen who looked like a younger version of her mother, had suitors every evening and on Sundays as well. Sporting pocket watches and singing the latest popular hits, they were so obvious in their attempts to impress the girl that I had to leave the kitchen and laugh outside.

One Sunday, I was standing in front of the house talking to Hylek's cousin when I saw two German soldiers walking through the village street. They were plain Wehrmacht men and their walk was leisurely. They carried no weapons.

I no longer became frightened merely at the sight of a

German uniform. Perhaps I had played my role of Joseph Szalewski for so long that it had become a reality. Besides, I was legally registered.

Hylek's cousin said, "Joziek, why don't you ask these soldiers if they have cigarettes for sale?"

I have often recalled this moment. Incredible as it may sound, I had somehow acquired a facility with German by listening to my parents speaking in what was a second language in our home. My father was born and educated in Galicia, which, before the First World War, was part of the Austrian empire. My mother learned German in a Warsaw high school. When they wished to converse without letting the children know what they were saying, they spoke in German. Of course, I had somehow learned enough to understand what they were saying. But I myself had never spoken German.

Whether I wanted to oblige Hylek's cousin or face a new challenge, I have never fully understood. But there I was, walking over to the soldiers and asking them, "Have you, perhaps, cigarettes for sale?"

The soldiers stopped. One of them answered, "What can you give me for them?"

"What would you like to have?"

"Oh," said the soldier, "eggs, butter… Have you got any?"

"I can get some."

"Good," said the soldier, "come over in an hour and bring some eggs and butter. We're over there." He pointed to the estate at the foot of the village. "Ask for Franz. That's me." He pointed to himself.

"Good," I said, and the soldiers walked away.

Hylek's cousin was excited. He kept on repeating, "What did he say? What did he say!" He accepted my ability to communicate with Germans without question. After all, I was a "city boy."

I told him, "He asked me to see him in an hour and bring some eggs and butter. He will trade the food for the cigarettes."

Cigarettes were expensive and hard to find in the village. Hylek's cousin was a habitual smoker. He thought for a moment. "I will sell you a dozen eggs and a half kilo of butter," he said, "if you sell me the cigarettes that you get from the Germans. Agreed?"

"Agreed," I said, "but I haven't any money right now."

"That doesn't matter. You'll have the cigarettes when you come back." And he went to the house to get the eggs and butter.

As I entered the grounds of the estate, I saw soldiers in front of the mansion. There was a large tent under tall trees. Six medium-sized tanks were half hidden in black earth dugouts, camouflaged by tree branches. The soldiers, scattered over the area, some in their undershirts, were washing, shaving, or standing around talking. A soldier came over and asked me what I wanted. I told him I was looking for Franz. He called out, "Franz! Someone wants to see you!"

Franz was standing behind a tank, unpacking a rucksack. He waved his hand, indicating that he wanted me to come over. It turned out to be a profitable transaction. I received fifty booklets of Pyramiden cigarette paper for the dozen eggs and three packages of cut tobacco for the half kilo of butter.

Back home, I sat down on my bunk and, using the lowest market price, calculated that I owed Hylek's cousin twenty booklets of cigarette paper and one pack of tobacco. He was happy, and felt he'd been paid a good price for his products.

The last time I'd felt free, the last time I'd felt the burden of German occupation lifted from my spirit was when I was smuggling candies into the Warsaw Ghetto during the fall of 1940, almost four years earlier. Doing things prohibited by the enemy countered the enemy's will, and was the essence of freedom. Yes, freedom from fear. Then and there I knew I would continue to follow my spirit's desire to be free of fear. If my body survived but my soul were destroyed by fear, it would mean that the Germans had won. They, the Germans, had decreed that I was not a human being. That I had no right to freedom. That I had no right to life. I decided to continue proving them wrong.

I made enough money in that one afternoon to pay for my violin, and still had some left over. The next evening, I sold the rest of the cigarette paper and tobacco, and I found there was a demand among the villagers for all kinds of things besides tobacco and paper. Some people heard about the barter and eagerly asked me to buy soap, razor blades, and other hard-to-get merchandise for them. I bought a dozen eggs and a chunk of smoked bacon with the money I had earned on the first transaction.

I ventured into the estate again, carrying the food in a paper-mesh bag. The soldiers were sitting on and around the tanks. Franz called out, "Come here! I've got something to show you."

As I came closer, he climbed into his tank, emerging a minute later with a large bundle of clothes. Wrapped around it was a grey three-quarter winter jacket made of blanket material. Inside was an assortment of shirts, underwear, and socks, all crumpled together. The soldier put the bundle on the edge of the tank and waited for me to estimate its contents. Then, with an air of hopeful expectation, he asked, "What will you give me for it?"

"One dozen eggs and a piece of smoked bacon," I replied without a moment's hesitation. I tried not to think where the soldier got the stuff. Maybe he found it.

"Good!" said the soldier, and the deal was made.

I carried the bundle home, opened it, and spread the contents on the earthen floor of the shed. As I began sorting them, I felt a tingle running down my spine. It was a miracle! All the clothes seemed to be my size. The shirts were perfect at the neck and sleeves. The grey pants were so well fitted that I could wear them without a belt. I carried the bundle into the house and showed it to Mrs. Hylek.

She told me to leave it with her so that she could wash the clothes for me.

The next day, I could hardly wait to get back home with the cows. I hadn't had a decent shirt for a long time, and the pants seemed to be made of English material. The coat was heavy and warm, just the thing for the coming winter.

I wanted to share my luck with one particularly poor boy, a cowherd like myself. But for a cowherd to behave philanthropically in a small village like Godzice would not be sane, so I contrived a more subtle approach. Five neatly ironed shirts were waiting for me on the kitchen stool, along with four pairs of socks, four underpants, and my beautiful grey pants draped over the ironing board. My coat, still wet, was hanging on a line outside. I picked up two of the shirts, put them into the paper-mesh bag, and walked to the other end of the village.

The boy, Janek, was an orphan. He worked for the biggest farmer in the village. Actually, the farm was run by two obese, unmarried sisters and their brother. The parents of the trio were dead. Janek wasn't too well off there. The family was known for their tightness.

I walked into a large kitchen and greeted the two sisters: "*Dobry wieczor.* Good evening." The boy was sitting on a low stool, peeling potatoes. They made him do all kinds of things, those sisters.

"Did you get the thread?" asked the older sister. She had inquired about thread the previous evening.

"Not yet," I replied, "but I will try to get it for you." I approached the boy, who stopped peeling potatoes and looked up.

"Janek, I have a couple of good shirts for sale. They're your size."

The boy got up from the stool, excited. "Let's see them."

I held the shirts in front of him. He wanted to touch them, but his hands were wet. He wiped his hands on his worn pants and felt the material of one of the shirts. I could see that the boy wanted to have them. He looked anxiously at the older sister, seeking her approval. She gave him a "go ahead" look, and Janek asked, his voice quavering, "How much do they cost?"

The shirts were worth at least 200 zlotys each.

"One hundred and fifty apiece," I answered. Janek looked at the older sister with pleading in his eyes. She hardened her jaws.

"I will give you 125 apiece!" blurted out Janek desperately. I felt sorry for him, but his timidity angered me.

"I will not take less than a 100 zlotys apiece," I stated firmly.

Janek almost jumped. The older sister looked stupefied. Janek turned towards her. "Could you give me my money?" he asked, too determined to be afraid of her. She reached into her apron pocket and took out a large handkerchief tied into a knot. Still confused, she counted out 200 zlotys from a thick wad of bills.

The next day, I went over to the estate. The soldiers were

gone. Black holes in the ground where the tanks had been were the only evidence of their two-day sojourn.

Life went back to "normal" for a while. I drove the cows to pasture every day and played my violin, learning Latin at odd intervals. Dressed in my new clothes, I went to church the next Sunday and walked carefully, avoiding puddles of water along the way. Autumn had come, and it had rained the night before.

The village *soltys*, a poor farmer who acted as the reeve to supplement his income, came to Hylek's house the next morning and informed them of the latest German ordinance. Every farm had to supply a man one day a week to work on the construction of tank-trap ditches. The men, he said, would be picked up at seven o'clock every morning by a train passing on a railway line near the village. They would be taken in boxcars to the district town, Sochaczew, and brought back by the same train at the end of the day. After the *soltys* left, Mr. Hylek told me, "Joziek, you will go with the other men on Wednesday morning."

He added that there would be coupons redeemable for cigarettes and vodka provided by the Germans for the men working on the *Panzergraben*. I could keep the coupons I earned and redeem them myself.

It was still dark outside on Wednesday morning when the men met in front of the reeve's farm. We walked one kilometre to the railway tracks and waited in silence. There were twenty of us. After a while, a puffing locomotive trailed by a caterpillar of brown boxcars approached us and slowed down, grinding and hissing to a stop. We climbed into one of the boxcars, and the door slid shut. As the train pulled away and picked up speed, the greyish dawn peered in on the group of silent men through four dusty panes. At Sochaczew, we disembarked. I saw many more men jumping out of the other boxcars. A German civilian appeared on the platform and shouted to us in Polish to follow him. We walked about two kilometres to the outskirts of the city. There, the German ordered us to stop.

The fields around us were scarred by finished and partly finished deep, V-shaped ditches. Some of the ditches were lined with concrete. Triangular iron spikes, black and thick, were embedded on the sides and tops of the finished ditches. Farther on, I could see a row of wooden barracks. Men wearing brown uniforms and brown boots were walking between the barracks. The purpose of these ditches was easy to guess, even for someone untrained in military matters. These were formidable barriers, too wide and too deep for tanks to pass without throwing bridges across them.

Our group was led to an unfinished section of a ditch, where shovels, picks, and spades were distributed to us by another *Volks*-German. He spoke Polish, but with a German accent.

*Volks*-Germans were people who lived in Poland before the war as Poles, but considered themselves German and swore loyalty to Hitler as soon as Germany marched into Poland in September of 1939. They ostensibly had to provide some proof of German ancestry, but in reality almost any Pole, if he so desired, could become *Volks*-German. Those who did so were scorned and hated by the Polish people, hated even more than the German invaders.

As they worked, the men talked in monotones about the cursed *Volks*-Germans, their lips hardly moving. Their averted eyes disguised their scorn and contempt for the man who stood above them, watching their progress. I tried to determine in my own mind what kind of a man he was. He appeared to be about forty, harsh and cold and, I thought, insecure in spite of his commanding manner.

Each man in our group worked on a small portion of the ditch. I tried as hard as I could to complete my assigned metre-square section. Still, at the end of our working day as the sun was sinking, other members of my group had to help me out or our assignment would have been left unfinished and the whole group held responsible. They were good people and did the work without blaming me or hurting my feelings. But a couple of them were angry at Hylek for sending a boy to do a man's job, when he had a big strapping fellow, his son Wojtek, sitting at home.

Something totally unexpected occurred just before we climbed into the boxcar to ride back to Godzice. The men became uneasy as a drunk Wehrmacht officer, swaying to and fro, addressed them in German, asking questions about Zakopane. Zakopane was a resort area in the Carpathian Mountains and seemed to be his destination.

"You speak German, Joziek," one of the men prodded

me. "Ask him what he wants." The rest of the men in our group instinctively pulled back.

I faced the officer and told him that I could speak a little German. He brightened and immediately informed me that he was going to Zakopane. Guessing that he wanted to be complimented on his choice of destination, I told him, "Zakopane *gross*! Zakopane is *big*!" I opened my arms wide to emphasize how large it was.

The German was happy. "*Jaaaaa*! Zakopane *gross*!" he repeated after me. "Zakopane *gross*!" He staggered away, reassured and satisfied but still stone drunk. The men heaved a sigh of relief and patted me on my shoulder.

Back home in my bunk, tired, my muscles aching and my hands blistered, I fell asleep at once.

The next day when I came back from the pastures, I saw German soldiers walking through the village street. A company of Wehrmacht had been stationed in the village. Two of the Germans were quartered in Hylek's house. They were given the "private" living room. I was called in to act as an interpreter between the Hyleks and the new occupants.

I soon found out that one of them was the company's *Zahlmeister* (paymaster) and the other one described himself as a *Marketenderwarenmann*, that is, the man in charge of the sale of small articles such as cigarette paper, lighters, toothbrushes, and other items not freely provided to the soldiers of his company. The *Marketenderwarenmann* was a short, fat, jolly man in his late thirties. He was quick in his movements and had blue eyes and a balding forehead. The

*Zahlmeister* was long and thin, with red hair and brown spots on his skin. He was a sad-looking family man. He told me about his wife and two daughters who lived in Hannover. He missed his dear ones. His watery blue eyes became more watery when he talked about them.

The next evening, after I ate my dinner, the fat, jolly one came out of his room and motioned to me to follow him outside. He went behind the house and I followed him, wondering what this was about. The man looked around, to make sure that no one was watching us.

"Joseph," he whispered, "I need Polish money. I have some things to sell. Would you be interested?"

"What do you have for sale?"

He reached into the right side-pocket of his uniform jacket, and produced two automatic cigarette lighters. They had blue enamelled sides and chrome tops and bottoms. I knew that a good cigarette lighter was worth a couple of hundred zlotys. I asked, "How much do you want for these?"

The man started to count in his head, talking aloud in fragments: "A mark is 2 zlotys…20 marks…that's 40 zlotys."

He completed his mental calculations and faced me. "Forty zlotys apiece," he proposed, a bit uncertainly, as if afraid that he was asking too much. I counted out four twenties.

"Good," I said, as I handed the money to the *Marketenderwarenmann* and received the cigarette lighters. I sold one to a village farmer for 150 zlotys and kept the other for myself.

The same thing happened the following evening, only this time I bought two boxes of Pyramiden cigarette paper, each containing fifty booklets. The *Marketenderwarenmann* had asked 20 zlotys for each box. I sold them without difficulty for 10 zlotys per booklet. My capital was now accumulating. I had well over 1,000 zlotys. By now, the people in the village were asking for all kinds of things. However, demand for tobacco products remained predominant.

A soldier who stayed in another farmhouse had heard about my business. He came to see me the following evening. He waited in front of the fence and called me when he saw that I had finished putting the cows in their stalls.

"Hey, boy!" I walked over to meet him. "I hear you're buying things," he whispered, with an expression of eager expectation on his face.

"Oh, sometimes," I replied cautiously, and inquired casually, "Why?"

"I have a few things I want to show you," said the private, and added, "Can you come over to where I'm staying?"

"Sure," I answered, and went with him to the fourth farmhouse from Hylek's. The soldiers there were quartered in a barn, which we entered. There were two more soldiers lying on the straw, covered with blankets. One of them, a hefty but tired-looking fellow, had a red-celluloid chromatic accordion with a pearly finish lying by his side. I tried not to let my excitement show, and waited for the soldier who had brought me to speak.

The man bent over his knapsack and took out five packages of tobacco. He held them in front of me. "How much will you give me for it?" he asked, and explained, "I don't smoke, and Polish zlotys can be changed into marks."

The tobacco was worth 50 zlotys a package and I could sell a hundred of them if I had them. "How much do you want?"

"Five marks...that is, 10 zlotys for one package."

I paid him 50 zlotys and took five packages. "Wait," said the soldier, "I have something else." The other soldiers were getting up, curious about the activity in progress.

While the tobacco seller went back to his knapsack, the big fellow with the accordion came over to me and asked, "Do you also buy clothes? Or only tobacco?"

"I buy anything I can sell."

The soldier nodded and returned to his place on the straw. I had the feeling that he was afraid to do business in front of the others. The man sat down on the edge of a wooden enclosure, picked up his accordion, and tried to play a song, which I recognized. He couldn't really play. The tobacco seller came back, holding other items: two packages of cigarettes and a handful of cigarette-paper booklets. I bought everything. Meanwhile, the accordion player was getting disgusted with his own inability to play. As he started to remove the straps from his shoulders, I asked him if I could try playing his accordion. The soldier obliged, handing me the shiny box. I put in on and started investigating the system it used.

A chromatic accordion plays a different note when it is pulled apart than the note it plays when pressed together. I discovered that it was almost the same as playing a harmonica, with the additional left-hand basses and chords to watch. These had a chromatic arrangement as well. In about three minutes, I played the very song the soldier had attempted to play. The soldiers were surprised and glad to be entertained. Encouraged, I tried other songs and played them with equal success. When I stopped playing, I asked the soldier if I could borrow his accordion for a while. He said I could have it for two hours.

I went home with the accordion slung over my shoulder, my newly acquired merchandise securely hidden in the cuffs of my pants. First, I hid the merchandise in the straw of my bunk. Then I sat on the bench in front of the house to play the accordion. The music brought the two Germans out of the living room, and the Hyleks from the kitchen.

They all laughed, and the *Zahlmeister* said that this called for a celebration. He went back to his quarters and came out holding a bottle of cognac. He asked Mrs. Hylek for glasses, and she understood him without any need for interpretation, which again made everybody laugh. Everyone, except Hylek's daughter and Bronek, had a drink, and I played for the full two hours.

When, after returning the instrument, I came back home, the fat, jolly soldier was waiting for me. It was almost dusk. He was holding a parcel larger than ever before. In it was an assortment of military-issue items. One by one, he took out samples of the items. "These are gasoline bottles for refuelling cigarette lighters. Can you use them?"

I could use them. I could also use the three toothbrushes, six imitation leather wallets, and fifty booklets of cigarette paper. The *Marketenderwarenmann* pocketed the money, satisfied. With the exception of Wednesday, when I again spent the day digging ditches in Sochaczew, my business activities imposed such a demand on my time that I paid 20 zlotys a day to one of my cowherd friends to take care of my cows. He passed by with his cows each morning and drove my cows to the pastures along with his small herd, then brought them back at the end of the day.

Mr. Hylek was confused by all this. Germans in his "private" living room. He had to sleep in the kitchen with his sons, three in one bed, while his wife slept in the small back room with their daughter. I, his cowherd, was contracting the pasturing of his cows to other cowherds. And to top it all, he was all out of tobacco! These changes left him in a position for which his lifelong habits had certainly not prepared him. He grumbled to himself under his skimpy mustache, but finally came to me to buy tobacco and cigarette paper. I gave him a special discount price. With the cows off my hands, I was able to do business all day long, and became ever more known to the soldiers and the farmers alike.

A soldier patrolled the village road every night now. One night, my business activities held me up at a farmer's house until late. Walking back home I heard a shout: "*Parole! Password!*" coming from just ahead of me on the road. I stopped, and in murky darkness saw the silhouette of a German soldier holding a rifle, which was pointed at me. I improvised. "Joseph *geht*! Joseph goes!" I shouted as quickly as I could.

The soldier, his rifle still pointed at me, approached slowly. I recognized him as one of my best customers. "You shouldn't walk around at night like this!" he said seriously. "I could have shot you!" He seemed to be more shaken than I by the encounter. He hung the rifle on his shoulder and waved me on.

In truth, reinforced by my recent success in business, my self-confidence had soared, eliminating any semblance of fear from my mind. I felt alert and quick to judge any situation.

As I started to leave, the soldier called after me: "Joseph!" I stopped and turned around. The watchman walked over and said, "I just remembered I have a message for you from the *Oberst's* [colonel's] *Ordonnanzoffizier*, Franz. He wants to see you."

"Thank you," I said. "I'll see him tomorrow. *Gute Nacht.*"

"*Gute Nacht,*" answered the soldier, resuming his patrol through the dark village street.

Early the next morning, I ventured to see Ordonnanz Franz, as he was called. He was at the headquarters of the company. Since the house was occupied by only a childless couple, two rooms had been requisitioned by the Germans. The first room was used as office, kitchen, and Ordonnanz Franz's bedroom. The second room served as the *Oberst's* bedroom. I walked in and greeted the two men in the room:

"*Guten Morgen.*"

"*Guten Morgen,*" they returned my greeting.

The *Oberst*, a short, corpulent man of about fifty, almost bald except for greying fringes, was sitting at a table, which also served as a desk. There was a partly eaten fried egg and a slice of bread on his plate. Surrounding the plate were an inkwell, a pen holder, and two pads of paper. Ordonnanz Franz was standing by a small iron stove. Along the far wall stood a portable iron bed with a military-issue blanket.

Franz was thin and slightly taller than the *Oberst*, but his peculiar posture made him look smaller. He was bent almost like a hunchback. His sparse hair was of a nondescript colour. His steel grey eyes were shrewd and untrusting. There was something repulsive about the man. He served the *Oberst* a large mug of steaming brew and then looked towards me.

"I was told you wanted to see me," I said a bit stiffly.

Franz looked at the *Oberst*, as if waiting for him to speak. The *Oberst* wiped his mouth with a large handkerchief.

"You speak German well. Where did you learn it?" he said, with a slight a smile on his face.

"I learned it from my mother. She took it at school as a second language," I was trying to appear as relaxed as possible. The *Oberst* nodded approvingly. He didn't ask any more questions. He knitted his brow and looked up at Franz, who gave me a crooked imitation of a smile and said,

"You are doing some business, I heard, changing cigarettes for food?"

"Oh, yes, if someone wants to..." I said casually, letting the unfinished sentence hang in the air.

"The *Oberst* wants some bacon," said Franz. "If you can get it, I will pay you with cigarettes or tobacco."

The *Oberst* was busy studying some papers. He held the mug in one hand and sipped the brew as he read.

"I will bring it to you this afternoon," I said, "but only a small piece. Bacon is hard to get. There isn't much of it around."

"Ha!" exclaimed Franz, with a shrug of his shoulders and a knowing look. "There's plenty of it, but it's hidden. We know."

I smiled. "I will try to get as much as I can."

Obtaining bacon from farmers was not easy. It mostly came from the slaughter of illegal pigs. Raising an illegal piglet was difficult and risky, and when the grown pig was slaughtered by the farmer, the farmer was reluctant to part with his only supply of pork.

I searched far and wide, going from one farmer to another until at the fifth place I tried I bought half a kilo of bacon. I went back to the *Oberst*'s office and presented it to them. Franz took a critical look at the bacon wrapped in a sheet of oily paper. After examining the bacon for a few moments, he decided that it looked all right. Now came the question of price. I asked for two packages of tobacco and got them.

This deal started a regular delivery service every third day. One day, I noticed a Polish-language newspaper on the table. It was the *New Warsaw Courier* (the *Warsaw Courier* before the war). I was starved for news, and asked if I could have it. My request was granted. What's more, Franz told me that since the paper was delivered every day, and no one at the *Oberst*'s office could read Polish, I could have all the issues.

From then on, I was well informed—that is, if a Polish paper controlled by the Germans could be considered a reliable source of information. The war news described German "strategic retreats" and "straightening out the lines," but one could easily see that the Germans were losing the war. It was only a question of time. Still, I dared not look forward or back. To let down my guard even for a moment could mean instant death. I lived in the present as an almost completely authentic Joseph Szalewski.

I made money every day and stuffed it into a woollen sock that didn't have a mate. I kept it under the straw mattress. Every night before going to sleep, I gave it a reassuring squeeze to check it was still there. I hoped that one day I would have enough money to buy an accordion. The opportunity came sooner than I expected.

A few new soldiers had been added to the company quartered in the village. The day the soldiers arrived, I was with the cows in the pasture. There wasn't enough business to justify my staying home and paying 20 zlotys to another boy to watch my little herd. After supper, I went out in front of the house to see if there was anyone looking for me. Standing there was a newly arrived soldier of medium height, a dry-looking man of about forty. He asked, "Are you Joseph?" When I answered in the affirmative, the soldier said, "I have an accordion for sale. Would you like to buy it?"

I tried to conceal my excitement and asked casually, "What kind of an accordion is it?"

"I don't know," said the soldier. "I can't play it."

"Where is it?" I asked. The soldier sounded like a Bavarian farmer. I'd heard the dialect before.

"Wait, I'll bring it right over."

"Good," I said, and waited. After what seemed like an hour but was probably only a ten minutes, I saw the soldier coming out of a distant farm and walking towards me. He was carrying a very small red accordion, holding it against his side. I was somewhat disappointed with the size of the accordion. As the soldier approached me, I counted the basses. Six bass buttons and six chord buttons—only major chords, no minors.

"Here it is," said the soldier, handing me the accordion. It felt good just to hold the accordion in my hands, it was so light.

"What do you want for it?" I asked, expecting a steep price of at least 500.

"I want Polish money. It's worth half of German money, so the price will have to be double," answered the man with a note of caution in his voice.

"How much?"

The soldier proceeded with the now familiar calculation:

"Seventy marks. That's 140 zlotys." I paid him.

He was back the next day, complaining that Polish money wasn't worth much. He'd sold the accordion for too little, he said. I pointed out that I'd paid him what he'd asked. The soldier couldn't refute that, and went away mumbling about Polish money being useless.

And so I had my first accordion. I took it along to the pastures and played all the melodies that were in major keys, and some in minor keys, but those I played without the left-hand chords, which were strictly major. All the boys and girls watching their herds in the pastures gathered around me that day and took turns bringing my cows back when they wandered off.

Glancing up between songs, I saw my previous employer, Jan Zdziech. He was sitting on a huge boulder, resting his chin on one hand and listening to the music. I was glad that he could hear me now. Later, after I got back home, I met a boy from Stanislawow who told me that Mr. Zdziech said that I was King of the Cowboys. It tickled my pride to hear that.

The following day was a Sunday and I sat in front of the house playing my accordion. The *Marketenderwarenmann* was standing close by, listening. Suddenly, two Germans wearing orange-brown uniforms and black ties, each holding a heavy leather whip in his right hand, walked into the yard. They headed straight towards me.

"Why aren't you at work, digging *Panzergraben*?" yelled one of them, and started to lift his whip.

"He works on the *Panzergraben*! I know he does! I see him go to work all the time. He is home today only because it is Sunday!" All this was rapidly spoken by the *Marketenderwarenmann*, who stood white-faced between me and the German with the whip. He kept on talking as if his own life were at stake.

The two SA men (I found out later that's what they were) looked at the man mockingly. The soldier was at least a head shorter than either of them.

To me, at that moment, he was a heroic figure standing up against the bullies. He was afraid. His hands were shaking. I looked at the SA men. There was cold, cynical cruelty in their faces and derision for the little soldier who was defending a mere Polish boy. "Haven't you anything else to do than to watch what he is doing?" said one of the SA men to the soldier. Then he swished the air with his whip and walked away, giving the soldier one last mocking, scowling look. His companion followed him out. I let out a deep breath and glanced at the *Marketenderwarenmann*. He could not look into my eyes and made an indecisive motion as if not knowing which way to turn. Then he walked out onto the street and disappeared from view.

Hylek's older son, Wojtek, staggered into the yard. His face was pale and distorted, and his walk was peculiar and wayward. He walked into the house without looking at me. After a moment, there was a commotion inside. I could hear Mrs. Hylek talking loudly to Wojtek, asking questions, and Wojtek answering in a broken voice. After a few minutes, Mrs. Hylek came out of the house carrying a pair of men's long underwear wrapped into a bundle. She filled a small basin with water from the pail at the well-crane and started washing the underwear. I asked her what had happened, and I added that there had been some Germans here with whips in their hands.

Mrs. Hylek said, "They caught Wojtek at our cousin's house. They asked him why he wasn't working at the ditches. Then they took him outside and told him to lie down on the spikes of the harrow. They were going to whip him. He ran. He was so scared that he filled his pants." She stopped and wrung out the garment, hung it on the line, and went back into the house.

After that, there was a marked change in atmosphere between the Hyleks and the two soldiers quartered in their house. Following Wojtek's frightening experience, the Hyleks tried to avoid any contact with the soldiers. I could not think of any reason for changing my approach. One of them had saved me from a beating, or worse.

I decided that German soldiers were mortally afraid of their own enforcers, men like the whip-bearing SA men. I pursued my business activities as before, with the exception of Wednesdays, when I dug ditches in Sochaczew alongside the other men of the village of Godzice.

The following Wednesday, after finishing our day's work at the ditches, we each received coupons for cigarettes and vodka redeemable at a special *Kontingent* store in Sochaczew. We went there as a group before boarding the train home.

I'd collected three coupons, which translated into a litre of vodka and 150 Junaki cigarettes, a Polish brand.

I was beginning to smoke. It made me feel grown up. I didn't inhale, just let the smoke drift out of my nose and mouth. Mrs. Hylek warned me against smoking. She said that later I wouldn't be able to stop, just like Mr. Hylek. Of course, she was right, but I didn't heed her warning and kept on puffing away.

After returning from Sochaczew, I strapped on the accordion, took my bottle of vodka under my arm, and walked to a narrow strip of grass between the fields, a short-cut to Mr. Glina's place. I came to pay off my debt and I hoped to hear Mr. Glina play his accordion, and perhaps to play along with him.

I handed Mr. Glina the 300 zlotys and set the bottle on the table. He came to life. "Magda! Bring in the glasses!" Mrs. Glina responded quickly and cheerfully. It seemed that she, too, liked a glass of vodka. After the first round, Mr. Glina brought out his accordion. It was beautiful! A 120-bass instrument covered in pearly white celluloid, intricately decorated with shiny red, white, and green rhinestones, which were set in patterns of flowers, bows, and zigzags.

Mr. Glina began to play. He played well. I listened intently, and after a while I tried to play along on my own little accordion. Unfortunately, the tuning was different. So we played alternately and drank together. Mrs. Glina was called to the little table during each round to join in the toast. Soon, the bottle was empty and the spirits were high. I staggered back home through the fields, my only difficulty being staying on the narrow strip of no-man's land.

When at last I reached home, I climbed onto my bunk and fell asleep at once, clothes and all. In the morning, I faced two consequences: a headache and the anger of the Hyleks. Why hadn't I stayed here? Why did I have to go to Glina to empty my bottle? It was only hinted, but very clearly so. I wasn't feeling well all morning, so I paid another boy to take my cows.

Later that afternoon, I went to see a *Feldwebel* (sergeant) who was quartered in a small house at the edge of the village, almost kitty-corner the solitary village store. The house belonged to a widow whose married son lived elsewhere. Besides the widow, the only other occupant of the house was the German *Feldwebel*. I had done business with him before. This day my objective was a sleeveless sheepskin jacket. I had seen it during my previous visit, but did not buy it because I ran short of cash after purchasing other, sure-profit items. With winter approaching, I wanted the jacket for myself.

A soldier stood in front of the house, and greeted me: "*Guten Tag*, Joseph."

"*Guten Tag*. How goes it?"

"Good," answered the soldier, and said, "Listen, Joseph, are you going to see the *Feldwebel*?"

"Yes," I answered.

The soldier came closer. He had a conspirator's expression on his face, like someone about to tell a secret. "Do you know that today is the *Feldwebel*'s twenty-fifth wedding anniversary?"

"No," I answered, "I must congratulate him." The door wasn't locked, so I walked right into the house. The *Feldwebel* was sitting on a small ottoman with the widow beside him. She was a plumpish woman of about forty with a round face and a huge bosom. Her brown hair was tied back. She liked to laugh, and needed little provocation to let go with a cascade of giggles. My mind was on business, but I wanted to be polite. "Congratulations on your twenty-fifth wedding anniversary, *Herr Feldwebel!*" I exclaimed with sincerity (for the sake of good business relations).

Just then, I noticed that the man's arm was around the woman's back, and I had the feeling that I had said the wrong thing, or perhaps the right thing, but at the wrong time. The *Feldwebel*'s arm went limp and shrank lifelessly back to his side. He looked unhappy. He was in his late forties, short, with a pudgy nose, a lined face, and a balding head. His uniform jacket was crumpled right now. The woman laughed, got up, and left the room, still laughing. She had not understood what I had said. It was just her nature to laugh all the time. The *Feldwebel* let out a deep breath, and smiled.

"*Danke schön*. Well, Joseph, have you got the money for the jacket?

"Yes," I started counting out the small wad of zlotys. I paid a comparatively high price for it, but it was worth it. The sheepskin jacket, worn with the wool on the inside, would keep my chest warm. I wasn't going to freeze this coming winter, as I had the past two winters for lack of warm clothing.

One morning a few days later, while it was still dark outside, I was wakened by Mrs. Hylek. I was half asleep and thought, Off I go to dig ditches again! But it wasn't that.

"Wake up, Joziek! Wake up! A German wants to see you!"

"A German?" I asked, instantly wide awake.

"Yes!" exclaimed Mrs. Hylek, with impatience, "The one who has the accordion...the one with all the buttons!"

I lifted myself up on my elbows. Seeing that I was awake, Mrs. Hylek left. I dressed quickly and went over to the neighbouring farm where the soldier was quartered. He and his two companions were packing their knapsacks in the barn. They were fully dressed and appeared tense and nervous. Something was up, I thought, as I watched the scurrying soldiers for a moment. Their usually relaxed faces were serious and drawn. "*Guten Morgen,*" I said, trying to start a conversation.

"*Ja, guten Morgen,*" answered the soldier who owned the chromatic accordion. His companions didn't return my greeting.

"Do you want to buy some stuff?" asked the soldier. "For Polish money," he added. With a bitter note in his voice, he announced, "We're going to the front."

So that was it! The soldier wanted to have money, Polish money, to buy civilian clothes and throw away his uniform, rather than be taken prisoner by the Russians. I'd overheard scraps of conversation between German soldiers while I was among them during my daily rounds of buying and selling.

"What kind of stuff?" I asked. The soldier picked up a pair of high rubber boots and held them in the air. Their black, shiny splendour, with red trim on top, toes, and heels, seemed out of place in the barn.

"Six hundred zlotys." He knew what to ask for those boots. The market price would be a 1,000 zlotys, perhaps. He put them down on the earthen floor.

"What else?" I inquired with an air of indifference.

The soldier took out a pair of German Wehrmacht boots, brand-new, nails and all, and set them alongside the rubber boots. "Twelve hundred," he said. He reached into his knapsack and pulled out a green long-sleeved sweater. The sweater was also new and also military issue. He held it in his hands for a moment, undecided what to ask for it.

"Three hundred," he finally said. He put the sweater on top of the knapsack and picked up his chromatic accordion by the straps, dangling it in the air. "You can have the accordion, too, for 1,200 zlotys."

"That's all?"

"That's all."

I did not haggle about the prices. They were relatively high, but I knew that I could still make a profit on these items. I went home to pick up the money, and returned to conclude the deal. The soldiers were ready to leave. They were waiting for a wood-burning truck to pick them up.

These smelly wood-combustion vehicles were used when there was a shortage of gasoline.

One of the soldiers made a joke: "You must be a half Jew, Joseph."

I laughed. If he only knew that I was a *whole* Jew!

The other soldier commented with irony, "We're going to collect a ration of ten cigarettes a day at the front. Still, I'd rather make out with four cigarettes a day and stay here!"

I understood him perfectly. Things were not too good for the Germans, especially at the front. According to the latest issue of the *New Warsaw Courier* from the *Oberst*'s office, the Russians were just across the Vistula River. They had held their position there since the summer of 1944, even before the Polish uprising. It was to be expected that sooner or later they would initiate an offensive and drive the Germans out of Warsaw. In an attempt to offset the unpleasant news, the German-controlled newspaper covered the front page with glowing accounts of the effectiveness of the German V-1 and V-2 pilotless rockets, which were used to bombard English cities, London in particular. I had my own thoughts about the German dreams of a "thousand-year Reich," which I kept to myself, with one somewhat careless exception. Later that day I told one of the lower-ranked officers in the village that "you need a lot of iron in order to build those V-1 and V-2 rockets!"

He was bragging too much about the damage inflicted by these pilotless bombs on the British people. Somewhat stumped by my negative statement, he replied, "Bah! Iron!" presumably meaning that the Germans had plenty of iron.

Once I had released my true emotions a bit, I found stopping difficult. I proceeded to quote the German soldier who preferred four cigarettes here to ten cigarettes daily at the front. However, I embellished the story by telling it in the plural.

"*Ach so!*" exclaimed the officer, his face turning a peculiar shade of crimson. "So, the German soldiers don't want to fight, eh?" He then took off his jacket and handed it to me. He started searching for pen and paper in his pockets, saying, "You take my jacket to my commanding officer! I will give you a note for him saying that I don't want to fight any more!" He found a small notebook and a fountain pen and started writing. I really didn't know how to get out of this situation. Things got out of hand and one thing was certain. The message I was to carry to his commanding officer, with his jacket, was definitely not his resignation from the Wehrmacht.

All this took place at a farmhouse where the under-officer was stationed. There were several people present—the farmer and his wife, and two men, one of whom was a visitor from the city. Fortunately for me he spoke German, and at this point he persuaded the under-officer that I was just a kid who didn't know what he was talking about. He may have saved my life. The message idea was abandoned. Instead, the under-officer focused his attention on the visitor, eyeing him with suspicion.

"You are of military age and you speak German," he spat out with bile. "Why aren't you in the army?"

The stranger was quick on the draw. "If I were," he said, "then I'd choose the SS." With these words he demolished the army under-officer's aggressive blustering by stressing the inferiority of the Wehrmacht compared with the SS. I shook the stranger's hand before I left for home. He smiled, and patted me on my shoulder. I would never see him again.

I looked over the items I'd bought earlier that day. I had decided to keep the rubber boots for myself. The sweater and shoes were for sale. I did not buy the accordion. It was a chromatic, and I had no use for it. The Hyleks were in the kitchen and I showed them my new acquisitions. Mr. Hylek was interested in the sweater for himself, and Mrs. Hylek called in her daughter to try on the shoes, which just happened to fit her. I let them buy both items at cost. They deserved it for being lenient with me and tolerating my business activities when I was supposed to have been taking care of their cows.

I was now prepared to meet the coming winter without freezing. The rubber boots would keep my feet warm in the coldest weather, especially when lined with fresh straw, which would help to absorb moisture and could be replaced every day. I could wrap my feet in rags from old flannel shirts and then put on the large German military-issue woollen socks over top. Luckily, the boots were large enough to accommodate all that.

The sheepskin jacket and the grey overcoat took care of
the upper part of my body, and a pair of black work pants
worn with the cuffs inside the boots completed the outfit.
The only thing still needed was head covering, and I came
across a good one the very next day. It was a lined, brown
leather cap, the same as those worn by German Luftwaffe
pilots. The earflaps could be snapped closed, and the cap
was extremely warm when the metal clamps at the chin-
straps were fastened together. I bought it from a German
truck driver for 50 zlotys.

November 1944 had arrived. The livestock were kept
inside now. Some soldiers had been moved out of the village, and others were assigned to their quarters. Drivers were
bringing in supplies for the company, using the smelly
wood-powered trucks.

I met a boy, a nice fellow my own age, who played the
violin like a professional. His name was Zbyszek. He was a
refugee of the Polish uprising in Warsaw. His father was
reported missing in action. His mother, a fine-looking, delicate woman, wandered from village to village with her son
after the uprising. Finally, they settled in Godzice, since one
of the farmers was a distant relative.

I was invited to play my accordion at a village party five
kilometres from Godzice. I accepted at a price of 500 zlotys, and took Zbyszek with me. We received another 250 zlotys in tips, and word spread through other villages that
there were two good musicians in Godzice. It being the
Carnival season right after Christmas, parties were plenti-

ful, and for the next few weeks we were kept busy playing two, three times a week. I shared the money fifty-fifty with Zbyszek. We gained more and more experience playing dance music. Sometimes we had to stay overnight in villages where we played because of the danger of walking after dark. Polish partisans moved from forest to forest. A German night patrol was killed in Godzice. Ever since then, it was risky to walk at night, even for me.

Then, on the morning of January 18, 1945, I was wakened by Mrs. Hylek. "Joziek! Joziek! Get up! The Germans are gone! People are going over to the highway! The Germans left a lot of stuff there!"

I was on my feet in no time at all, running towards the main highway a couple of kilometres north of the farm. There I saw people walking among abandoned ammunition wagons, picking up knapsacks, blankets, and anything else they could find. I looked the situation over carefully, and came to the conclusion that being able to pull a loaded ammunition wagon was far superior to carrying the loot on my back. It would also multiply by tenfold the amount of cargo I could haul away. And there was an abundance of goods scattered in fields and ditches on either side of the highway.

I examined a two-wheeled metal ammunition wagon, painted in a camouflage pattern. It was designed to be pulled by one horse. It had two metal pipes where the horse was supposed to be. Two pneumatic rubber wheels, revolving on a wheel-bearing axle, would minimize friction and make it fairly mobile. There was plenty of room in the rectangular hold-box. I tried to move it. It was easy! My mind was made up. I packed the wagon full of blankets, knapsacks, and anything else of value that I could find and pulled it towards the highway.

Then I saw the Russians! There was a column of cavalrymen coming, perhaps forty or fifty. The horses were walking, not even trotting. The men waved at me and laughed as they passed by. I waved back. The Germans were really gone! I couldn't believe it until I saw the Russians.

That meant I could go back to Warsaw! No one would want to kill me because I was a Jew!

But first, there was a job to be done—getting the wagon to the farm. I got stuck in a ditch and couldn't pull the wagon up out of it. I saw a woman walking nearby, carrying a bundle on her back. Spotting a pair of panties in one of my newly acquired knapsacks, I called out for help, waving the underwear as incentive. She helped me get the wagon out of the ditch, and I rewarded her with the panties.

Pulling the wagon along the frozen furrows of plowed fields, I arrived at the rear of the shed, which was filled with bundles of straw and hay. I opened the rear gates and pulled the wagon into the shed. The Hyleks came to admire my spoils. However, both they and I were somewhat disappointed when we opened the knapsacks one by one, and most of them turned out to contain only a dirty towel, a used toothbrush, and a shirt or two. There was an old pocket watch in one, a cheap fountain pen in another, some socks, underwear—that was all. The grey blankets were worth more; there were sixteen of them. Customers for them were found the very same day, and I sold most of the other stuff within a week.

When I counted the money stashed away in the sock, I found that I had accumulated a total of 70,980 zlotys. I had the violin I'd bought from Glina, my small accordion, a good and ample wardrobe, and a vehicle to transport all my possessions. I was returning to Warsaw!

A farmer from a nearby village who was going to Warsaw the following day agreed to let me tie my vehicle to the rear of his horse-drawn wagon. I said good-bye to the Hylek family and to my numerous friends in the village of Godzice and left early in the morning, my vehicle trailing behind the farmer's wagon. I was warmly dressed, sitting on top of my possessions, full of new hopes for what lay ahead of me.

I did not divulge my true identity to anyone in the village except Zbyszek, my musician friend. Why? I do not know. It could be that the transition from Joseph Szalewski to Arthur Schaller needed a little time.

On the way to Warsaw, I asked the farmer who towed me and my ammunition cart to stop briefly in Otarzew, just long enough for a visit to the Dahlen family. They were happy to see me still alive, and I was glad to see they were well. I had some small gifts, which I gave them, and then resumed our journey.

In my wallet was a slip of paper with an address written on it. Cecylia Sniegocka Street, No. 7. That was the address of an apartment building in the suburbs of Warsaw where Zbyszek and his mother lived. Several days earlier, before they left the village, they invited me to stay with them upon my return to Warsaw. That was my destination for the time being.

I felt elated with my new freedom, but a cold foreboding of what I could expect to find in Warsaw gripped my breast. I tried to push away the horror of what had happened in Warsaw during two uprisings by recreating images of my family—my parents, my brother, and myself—celebrating my triumphal return to Warsaw. I saw us laughing about my "chariot," loaded with the spoils of war—booty, looted from our enemy. Relishing the victory—the survival. Joking about the dangers of the recent past! Yes, for a moment I imagined myself to be a victorious emperor re-entering his domain in triumph!

The clip-clop of the horse's hooves interrupted my fantasy. This was not a victory celebration. My ammunition cart was not a chariot, and my spoils were insignificant. I was not a returning emperor—just a Jewish boy who was going back to the city of his birth after a long absence.

# part four

———

DURING MY BRIEF STOP IN OTARZEW, I MET A JEWISH officer in the Red Army who was a guest of the Dahlens. He told me about the Jewish Committee in Warsaw. On my return to the city, after locating Zbyszek's apartment and unloading my wagon, I made my way to the address the officer had given me.

On the second floor of the apartment building at 33 Targowa Street, I found a door with a sign: the Jewish Committee of Warsaw. After hesitating for a moment, I knocked. There were sounds of footsteps and of a key turning in the lock. When the door opened, a middle-aged man with a sad, kind face and sharp, intelligent eyes looked out at me.

"*Dzien dobry*," I said. "I am a Jew."

"Please come in," answered the man without a change in

his expression. He stepped aside to let me by. I walked in and looked around the large room. The wallpaper was yellow with age and stained in places. The furniture consisted of a counter, a filing cabinet, and a couple of wooden chairs. A woman stood behind the counter and another man was standing near a window. The impression was that of an apartment that was either newly occupied or soon to be vacated. I walked over to the counter and spoke to the woman.

"*Dzien dobry*. My name is Arthur Schaller. I am a Jew. I escaped from the Ghetto in late August of 1942."

The woman looked at me and lifted her gaze to the man near the window. The man walked slowly towards me and stopped a few feet away. He looked me over from top to bottom and up again, studying my face intensely. Then he said, "How do we know that you are a Jew? Many non-Jews come here claiming to be Jews to qualify for food and clothing packages. How do we know you are a Jew? Have you any proof?"

I was stunned. For more than two years I had survived only by hiding the fact that I was a Jew, and now I had to prove that I was one! Still, it was a good feeling of sorts to know that now non-Jews were pretending to be Jews. But the man was waiting for an answer.

"I have no papers in my own name, if that's what you mean," I replied rather defensively.

"No, we don't expect you to have documents. Do you know any Jewish prayers?" asked the man, looking straight into my eyes.

"I remember two," I answered. "*Moideh ani*, the morning prayer, and the *Ma nishtanah*, the Four Questions I used to ask my father at the Passover Seder." The scene returned from the long-hidden depths of my mind, my heart, and my soul: my father reciting the Haggadah on Passover night; my mother worshipping with her eyes the man she loved; the gleam of candles; the warmth and security of a family celebration. Then came my own part of the service. I had practised the Four Questions for many weeks. I stood up and spoke: "Why is this night different from all other nights?"

"Let's hear the *Moideh ani* now," said the man.

With tears rolling down my cheeks, I started to recite the morning prayer: praising God and thanking him for being alive.

When I finished, the man put his hand on my shoulder and said, "One more thing. Are you circumcised?"

"Yes," I answered.

"Come with me to the other room," said the man. I followed him into an empty adjoining room and showed him that I was indeed circumcised. We went back to the office after that, where I gave all the particulars: my name, former address, and the names of all the family members I could remember. The woman at the counter wrote everything down.

Then she looked through a list of names and said, "So far, no one has inquired about you. But as soon as someone does, we will notify you." She registered me and told me to come by every two weeks to pick up my food and clothing parcels, which were sent to Poland by the American Jews.

I left the office and walked through the busy streets of Praga, the area of Warsaw that had suffered least from the ravages of war. Most of the houses were standing and relatively undamaged. I crossed the pontoon bridge, newly built by the Polish Engineering Corps of the Red Army. The Germans had destroyed all three of the bridges that once joined Praga to Warsaw. The majestic Kierbedzia Bridge had stood here; now, all that remained of its central span was a jumbled mass of twisted iron beams. I walked on, following several cleared paths, trying to locate Mirowska Street, where I had once lived with my family. Rubble obliterated the streets entirely, and I could not find my way. Where before there had been a city teeming with people, now there was only a desert of broken concrete and bricks. Empty sky stretched from one end to the other of what had been the Warsaw Ghetto. I never went there again.

Zbyszek was practising his violin as I walked into the apartment. He stopped playing and approached me, still holding the instrument under his chain.

"Well, Jozie—I mean, Arthur—have you found anyone?"

"Not yet," I replied. "I'm registered. If someone shows up looking for me, the Jewish Committee will let me know."

Zbyszek's mother walked in from the kitchen and asked the same question. I explained it to her as I had to Zbyszek.

"It will take time," she said consolingly. "Today is the third of February, not enough time for people to have come back."

She's right, I thought, it's only been two weeks since the Russians threw the Germans out of Warsaw. It will take more time. But I had the picture of the Ghetto ruins in my mind, and there were thoughts and feelings I did not want to recognize, let alone speak about.

Zbyszek's mother must have sensed my feelings and did not say any more about it. She too was waiting for someone—her husband, reported missing during the Polish uprising.

Early the next morning I went to see a man who worked in the Ministry of the Treasury. I had to change my savings into the new Polish currency. Officially, we were allowed to exchange a maximum of only 500 zlotys. This man had created a sideline by changing all the money that people he could trust brought to him. He charged 10 percent for this service, so my 80,000 zlotys shrank to 72,000 new zlotys after the exchange.

It was fortunate that I had this connection. Soon afterwards, the old money became altogether worthless. But even the new money had little purchasing value. A kilo of bacon, for example, cost 800 zlotys! Since I contributed money to the upkeep of the household, it became clear to me that with food prices that high, my money would not last long.

Then Zbyszek came up with an idea. Many of the bombed-out apartment buildings had coal cellars. If we could get into these cellars and load the coal onto my ammunition wagon and pull the loads to Praga, we could sell it there for 4 zlotys a kilo. It sounded good. We went out looking for buried coal cellars and found one that very day with four hundred kilos of hard coal under the rubble. After three days of digging, we transported it all to the Praga bridge, where we sold it. We spent the following four days looking for another coal cellar, but in vain. During the last day of our search, however, I found a willing customer for my ammunition wagon and sold it for a fair price. That ended the coal business. Money was still melting away faster than ever.

Two weeks passed. I went to Praga to inquire at the Jewish Committee and to receive the promised package from America. While climbing the stairs up to the Jewish Committee office, I came upon a group of men dressed in striped pants and jackets like prison uniforms. When I glanced at their faces, my blood ran cold. These people were starved, more starved than the dying children on the sidewalks of the Warsaw Ghetto had been. They were almost like skeletons. I could tell from their faces that they were Jews, and I stopped to ask them where they were from. Just then, one of the men started talking to another in the group in a language that sounded like Greek. I continued climbing without knowing what had frightened me away from speaking to them—the strange language or their terribly starved faces.

The door to the Jewish Committee was wide open and there was a lineup of five or six people in front of the office counter. I took my place in line and, as I did so, quickly scanned their faces, looking for anyone I could recognize. Anyone at all. I sighed. No one I knew. The last person I looked at was a woman of about forty dressed in a black winter coat and wearing a flowery kerchief so that I could not really see her face at first. Suddenly I recognized her. "Mrs. Kohn!" I cried out.

She turned and her eyes tried to place me. It took a few seconds for a gleam of recognition to appear. "Arthur!" she exclaimed in a surprised voice. She came over to me and took hold of my hands, squeezing them as a stream of words cascaded out. "Wait till Richard sees you! My husband too! I almost didn't recognize you!"

She kept on talking, asking about my mother. I told her that I hadn't found my family yet. She told me how she had survived by working as a Polish teacher with false documents, all the while keeping her husband hidden in the attic of her home. Their son, Richard, had false identity papers as well and had attended the Polish schools. She was planning to travel to Lublin to visit her husband in a few days. He was doing business there, but she and her son had a place in the suburbs of Warsaw.

While she related all this to me, the people ahead of us in line were taken care of, and she was next. Before turning to the woman at the counter, she said that she would wait for me and take me to see Richard. My turn came. The woman leafed through a file and said with a note of regret, "Sorry, no one has inquired about you, and there will not be any food packages from America this week. There has been a delay."

I left the office of the Jewish Committee with Mrs.

Kohn. She talked almost without pause, and I was thankful for her chatter—it took my thoughts off other matters. While she spoke, I reflected on how much she had changed. My memory was of a quiet, reserved lady whose husband owned a large shoe store on Elektoralna Street before the war, and then in the Ghetto.

She and my mother were friends. They had tried to bring their sons together so that we too would become friends, but I'd never liked Richard much. He was such a milk-and-cookie mother's boy. Later, in the Ghetto, my mother bought shoes in large burlap bags from the Kohns and sold them. That was how she had kept us from starving.

I was happy that the Kohns had survived the German occupation. If they had managed to survive, I thought, Who knows—maybe some of my family has survived as well.

We arrived at Mrs. Kohn's residence. Richard and I talked for a while. He was still a milk-and-cookie boy. Mrs. Kohn mentioned once again her forthcoming trip to Lublin, and my thoughts turned to my father's family in Galicia, near Lublin. They might have survived the war.

"I'd like to join you on your journey to Lublin, Mrs. Kohn," I said.

"I don't mind having you travel along, but do you have enough money for the trip?" I told her how much I still had, and she said that it should be enough. I agreed to come to her place the following day. From there, we would walk to the railway station.

I went back to the apartment and told Zbyszek and his mother what had transpired at the Jewish Committee. They understood my longing to find my family. I gave them some of my remaining money and packed a few pieces of clothing for the journey.

It was still dark when I left the apartment the next morning. I walked briskly towards the river. Snow squeaked under my shoes and freezing wind bit into my cheeks. I was warmly dressed in my grey three-quarter coat, a lined brown pilot's cap snapped under my chin, and a pair of woollen gloves. I wished I'd taken my high rubber boots instead of the thin leather shoes. My toes, frostbitten during my stay at the Bargiels, had begun to ache. I increased my pace and stamped my feet down harder to warm them up.

At last I reached the pontoon bridge. People were walking down the earthen dike towards the bridge. The lights of Praga shone across the Vistula River. I stopped, turned, and stood there for a moment looking at the dark skeletons of cremated buildings, their jagged crevices outlined against the grey, cold dawn. I shivered. Facing the lights of Praga once more, I continued on my way.

Mrs. Kohn opened the door of her little bungalow before I had a chance to knock. I looked up at the shingled roof, thinking, That's where she hid her husband—in the loft, under this roof. She must have developed a keen sense of danger about anyone approaching that door during the German occupation.

"Come in, Arthur, I'm almost ready to go. We have to

catch the ten-thirty train." Richard was sitting by the kitchen table, eating his breakfast.

Mrs. Kohn started to put on her coat. Her dark hair was short and full of silver threads. Her eyes had lost their softness. This was indeed a different Mrs. Kohn from the one I had known. My thoughts shifted to my mother. Where was she? Would I ever see her again? And Jerzyk, my brother...and my father, somewhere in the Soviet Union.

"I'm ready. Good-bye, Rys..." said Mrs. Kohn, as she leaned over her son to kiss him.

I held the door open for her as she walked through it still talking to her son, giving him last-minute reminders about housekeeping, safety, and shopping. It was a short walk to the railway station, and soon we were standing on the concrete platform waiting for the arrival of the Warsaw-Lublin train. There was a large crowd of men and women on the platform already. Many were walking to and fro, stamping their feet. Some were standing guard over their luggage. Mrs. Kohn kept talking about her son and husband. She did not expect me to participate in her monologue. I was grateful for that.

The train arrived and immediately there was a struggle at the doors of the compartments as people tried to push themselves into already crowded spaces. Knees, hands, and elbows, pieces of baggage held overhead—every kind of pressure was used to get inside, as the alternative was a six-hour wait for the next equally crowded train.

We managed to get ourselves inside a compartment

through sheer determination. Having only two relatively small pieces of luggage helped as well. There was a shrill whistle from the engine, and the train started to move with a hiss and a clank. We grabbed the straps to keep our balance. String nets overhead were loaded with baggage right up to the ceiling. A man got up from a wooden seat and motioned for Mrs. Kohn to sit down. She gratefully accepted. I hung on to the strap and listened to the ra-ta-ta-tat of the wheels.

The city of Lublin had been freed by the Russian army months before they had launched their offensive across the Vistula River. The first Polish Communist government had been set up in Lublin. This government, headed by President Bierut, moved to Warsaw in January of 1945, but many offices were still centred in Lublin. The Central Jewish Committee for all of Poland was one of them.

After we disembarked at the Lublin railway station, Mrs. Kohn gave me a slip of paper with the address of a hostel for men where I was to meet her and her husband. My immediate desire was to go to the Central Jewish Committee office and inquire about my family. It was late afternoon and I hoped to reach the office before it closed.

The city appeared to be relatively undamaged. It seemed unreal somehow, to walk through a city where the buildings showed age and wear, but not the violent damage of war, like the ruins of Warsaw. Lublin was much smaller than Warsaw, and drab and dirty. But walking through a city unchanged by the war gave me a feeling of normalcy, of not being forced to blindfold my emotions so as not to feel the pain.

I passed street vendors who were selling suit-lengths of cloth thrown over one arm while they gesticulated with the other, trying to attract buyers. I went by open market stalls displaying bread and vegetables. Small groups of men huddled in the middle of the sidewalk; money changed hands; financial transactions were performed in whispers. They were buying and selling American dollars.

At one corner of the market square was a street sign with the name of the street where the Central Jewish Committee was located. A few houses from the corner, I found the right number and walked up a flight of squeaky wooden stairs leading to a corridor with many doors on either side. A dark-haired teenage girl suddenly emerged from one of the doors.

"Where is the registration office?" I asked.

"Over there," said the girl pointing. She ran off as another girl appeared out of nowhere and chased after her. Laughing, they both disappeared at the end of the corridor.

A man wearing glasses with yellow metal frames and very thick lenses came out of a room. He was short and had a fringe of greying hair on his otherwise bald head.

"*Shalom,*" he greeted me in Hebrew.

"*Shalom.*" The man took a few steps towards me and smiled at me. "A Jew? You look like a goy."

"I know," I agreed, and added, "I came from Warsaw to look for my family."

"Oh, your family," echoed the man earnestly, and nodded a few times. "And where did they live, your family? In

Lublin?" He talked absent-mindedly, as if repeating a well-worn phrase. He spoke as one who knew the answers before the questions were asked.

"No," I replied quickly, "In Ulanow, close to Bilgorai."

The man looked at me with sadness for a moment, and then with distinct and deliberate slowness said, "There are no Jews in Ulanow or in Bilgorai any more."

"But how do you know?" I blurted out in desperation. "I will go there and find out for myself!"

"No. Don't go there," the man said quietly. "They will kill you."

"They?" I exclaimed. "Aren't the Germans gone?"

"The Poles, the ones who stole Jewish homes and businesses. They don't want to give them back. They will kill you," said the man with a sort of bitter patience, as if explaining an elementary fact to a child.

"Does that mean that everyone in my family is dead?" My fists tightened and my voice shook.

"No, we don't know yet. It's too soon to say. Some people have come back. Not many, some. And some escaped to Russia."

"My father escaped to Russia, to Lvov, in 1940," I told the man, waiting for reassurance, any reassurance at all.

"Then he is probably there, alive!" guessed the man, obviously pleased to be able to offer me some hope. I grabbed at that hope and held on to it with all my heart. My father, alive! I must find him! I must.

"The shoes you are wearing—they are worn out." He

scrutinized me from top to bottom. "I can give you a pair of American shoes. Come with me to the stock-room." He did not wait for an answer but started to walk along the corridor. I followed him and was presented with a pair of brand-new black shoes with rubber soles, made in America. The man's kindness helped to cushion the incomprehensible possibility that I was the only survivor.

I walked the same streets I had walked before, but now I knew that this city was no different from Warsaw. Although the buildings of Lublin had not been destroyed by bombs, I could feel the destruction of the human spirit everywhere I turned.

When I reached the hostel at the address given to me by Mrs. Kohn, her husband was waiting for me. He looked haggard and old for a man of forty, brightening for only a moment when he first saw me. He took me to a restaurant, where we met his wife. We ate supper, for which I paid my share at Mrs. Kohn's request. My money was almost gone, an embarrassing fact not overlooked my Mrs. Kohn, who offered to buy the blanket I had brought along for the journey. I sold it to her for 800 zlotys.

That night I slept at the hostel in a big room with seven other men. In the morning I discovered a hole in my pants at the right knee, as if it had been gnawed by a mouse or a rat. I said good-bye to Mr. Kohn, who told me that he and his wife would be leaving Lublin and returning to Warsaw in a day or two. There was no need for them to stay there any longer.

My journey back to Warsaw was even worse than the train ride to Lublin. Not only were the compartments crammed like sardine cans, but the outside of the train was covered with a jumble of clutching figures as well. Holding on to door handles, many of them sat on their luggage, which they had tied to the steps. There were people clinging to both sides of the train, and even balancing on the platforms between the cars. The roof was for the brave, and there were a lot of them—even families with children, their possessions spread out on the roof, shivering in the bitter cold.

I found a spot on one of the steps, tied my bundle to the step with my belt, and sat down on top of it. I made sure that the handle I was going to hold on to was secure and that the door was not going to fly open.

The train started to pull away from the station. After puffing its way slowly through a number of junctions, it picked up speed and left the city of Lublin behind. In the cold greyness of that early March morning, the freezing wind howled over the huddled, silent people and raised clouds of misty snow from the fields. The shrill whistle of the train reminded the passengers clinging to the outside of the train that although they froze in the bitter cold, it was hot steam that drove the train to its destination.

The train made a short stop at a snowed-in station. I longed to get off and find myself a warm drink but feared losing my spot. Instead, I stayed where I was and thrashed my arms vigorously to warm myself.

Later, the train passed through a tunnel, and an excited commotion and murmur arose among the people along the length of the train. The word went around from one to another: "A man fell off the roof!" The train kept going. It did not stop.

My immediate travel companion was a middle-aged man who looked like a farmer. He was wrapped in a black sheepskin coat with the fur facing inside and a fur hat. He periodically reached into his coat pocket and withdrew chunks of coarse rye bread, which he chewed slowly and methodically. A woman of perhaps thirty sat behind him. She had tied herself to an iron handle with a rope and sat on a cardboard suitcase, wrapped in her coat and kerchief. She began talking to another woman who was about her own age, and I gathered from their conversation that they were high-school teachers on the way to assume new teaching positions.

My neighbour seemed to have finally consumed all of his bread supply. Now he was carefully rolling a cigarette, putting a generous pinch of coarse tobacco from a leather pouch into a scrap of newspaper. Shielding his hands from the wind with his coat, he pressed his back to the train so as not to lose his balance. Fascinated, I watched as the man succeeded in rolling a cigarette and lighting it with a huge copper lighter.

At last, in the late afternoon, the train puffed into the Warsaw-Praga station. Crowds of passengers came to life, shouting, calling to each other, and passing baggage down from the roofs. I was cold, hungry, and really wanted to go home, but I stopped off at the office of the Jewish Committee and asked if anyone was looking for me. The answer was again negative.

At the apartment everything was the same. Thin strains of uninspired violin practice greeted my ears. A heavy curtain hung over the balcony door and a circle of light spread under a lampshade, reinforcing the impression of isolation from the outside world. Zbyszek's mother complained for the umpteenth time about the high prices of food.

My money supply was melting faster than the bacon, which now cost five new 100-zloty bills a kilo. American parcels promised by the Jewish Committee had not materialized. Zbyszek and I decided to stop by the office once more, with the hope that the American parcels had arrived at last. "No parcels," the clerk informed me sadly.

"I was a member of Hashomer Hatzair at the Gesia location. Have you had any inquiries from other members of the Faiwuszyc Choir or the Zionist organization?" I asked as a last resort.

"Have you met Antek?" the clerk asked, leaning towards me as he eyed Zbyszek with some suspicion.

"Zbyszek is my friend," I reassured him. "Who is Antek?" I inquired.

"Antek is his Resistance Movement name. His real name is Itzak Zuckerman." The clerk's voice and facial expression gave a clear indication of the respect and admiration he had for the man called Antek.

"Where is he now?"

"He's three doors away—here, on Targowa Street. You can usually find him at the restaurant on the second floor. That's his office."

I ran all the way, with Zbyszek right behind me. The place was dimly lit. Itzak Zuckerman was sitting at a small oval table writing on a notepad. A telephone was on the table to his right. He was bigger than I remembered him and had grown a mustache. He looked up from his work.

"Faiwuszyc Choir," I managed to blurt out.

"Do you need money?" Itzak asked, as he pulled out two 100-zloty bills and motioned for me to take them. "*Shalom*," he said.

"*Shalom*, and thank you," I replied.

On the street, Zbyszek remarked with amazement, "So that's how it is to be a Jew! They just see you, and they give you money!"

Carrying my violin under my arm, I left the apartment early the next morning. I'd decided to sell my violin, and common sense told me that the conservatory would be a good place to inquire about a prospective buyer. I knew that the Frédéric Chopin Conservatory was located on Vilenska Street in Praga. The secretary suggested that a Mr. Bebrysz might be interested, and she wrote down his address for me.

The man was not home, but just as I was about to leave the building I ran into a tall, heavily built man who walked with a limp and carried a viola wrapped in a protective cover under his arm.

I excused myself and asked, "Are you Mr. Bebrysz?"

The man turned and smiled at me. "Yes, I am Bebrysz," he said.

"Mr. Bebrysz, I have a violin for sale. I was told that you might be interested."

Somehow, I felt very embarrassed under the man's friendly stare. So much, in fact, that as I reached under my arm to show Mr. Bebrysz my violin, it slid out and fell with a clatter, while I stood helplessly holding the bow. My embarrassment even greater, I picked up the violin, and after seeing it was not damaged by the fall, showed it to the man.

"I'm sorry, but I'm not in the market for a student-type violin," said Mr. Bebrysz. "Are you a musician?"

"I play the accordion. My mother is a concert pianist."

"I cannot buy your violin, but I may be able to help you to obtain some financial aid," said Mr. Bebrysz. "Come to the office of the Musicians Association tomorrow morning." At this point, Mr. Bebrysz wrote down the address of the Musicians Association in a notebook, tore out the page, and handed it to me.

During our short meeting, I had developed a liking and feeling of respect for this man, and I was glad to see him the next morning. He was sitting behind a desk as I approached him.

"Good morning. Sit down," he said, shuffling some papers. "Now what is your name?"

"Arthur Schaller," I replied. Mr. Bebrysz lifted one eyelid and then half closed it in the next instant.

"Are you...a German?" he asked coldly.

"No, I am a Jew," I responded quickly. The question took me by surprise. Of course I knew that my family name sounded German. Still...

Mr. Bebrysz laughed heartily and started writing. "I am giving you a slip," he said. "If you go to the cashier next door, he will give you 500 zlotys."

I felt embarrassed. "Thank you," I mumbled.

"Don't thank me. This money is designated to help musicians. It does not come out of my own pocket," said Mr. Bebrysz, sensing my embarrassment. He stood up, shook my hand, and we parted.

After I collected the 500 zlotys from the cashier, I went to an employment agency. The girl at the agency said, "There's nothing for you now, but come back in three days."

Next, I went to the Frédéric Chopin Conservatory of Music and registered as a violin student. I was given a card with the address of a violin teacher, a Mr. Olenski. He gave lessons at his apartment, as many teachers did because of the shortage of rooms at the conservatory. Mr. Olenski turned out to be a nice but rather dry old man, who was occupying an anciently furnished apartment along with his wife and a cat. During the first lesson he kept bending my arm to correct my playing posture. Then he assigned a few exercises as homework, and the lesson was over.

Two days later, I stopped in at the employment agency again. The girl recognized me and smiled. She kept her word and presented me with not one but three job possibilities.

The first, she said, was construction work, rebuilding

the railway station, which had been destroyed by bombs. The second choice was to work as a cleaner in a government building, specifically, the Presidium Council of Ministers. The third choice was to clean old bricks and clear streets of rubble. I liked the sound of the job in the middle, and said so. The girl filled out a form and gave me the address: the corner of Vilenska and Targowa.

The day was cold but sunny. The streets of Praga were bustling as I made my way towards the government building complex. I stopped in front of the huge block of impressive six-storey structures. The wrought-iron fences that surrounded the complex formed circular and spiral patterns below, with spears ranged along the top. I approached the guard, a Polish soldier standing at one of the entrances with a carbine on his shoulder.

"I was sent here by the employment agency," I told the soldier, showing him my work form.

"You will have to go to the pass office and get a pass," said the soldier, pointing to a smaller building across the street. It was a few buildings away from the Frédéric Chopin Conservatory on Vilenska Street.

There was a long lineup of people waiting for passes. After a two-hour wait, I obtained a pass and entered the complex without difficulty. I was informed that the personnel department of the Presidium Council of Ministers was located on the sub-floor, and proceeded there directly.

The Communist government was encouraging people to stop using Mister, Miss, and Ma'am, in favour of the more politically correct Citizen. Still, most people continued to use the old forms of address. I received my first official rebuke from a woman in the personnel department, whom I had addressed as "Ma'am."

"We no longer use that term," she reprimanded me stiffly. "You will kindly address me as Citizen."

I did not argue. If the woman didn't want to be a lady, that was her business. I called her Citizen and got the job. My duties were as she described them to me: "to keep the main staircase clean and orderly."

I reported for work the following morning, showing my pass to the guard at the entrance. I was issued a push broom and a dustpan from the stockroom and promptly dispatched to work, along with a short, stocky, nervous-looking man with whom I was to share my duties.

We started sweeping on the top floor, the sixth it was, and worked our way down, each sweeping one side of the double grey-marble staircase. For lunch we went to the cafeteria on the top floor, where we could eat a full meal of soup, a main course, and a beverage for a reasonable price.

The rest of the day, until three-thirty, we patrolled the staircase and saw to it that it stayed clean despite the steady procession of people walking up and down. My partner's name was Wladyslaw, and he turned out to be a nice hardworking person. He was married and had an eight-year-old daughter.

Once a week I had a violin lesson and would go directly to the conservatory after work. I often practised at the

ministry as well. This routine of work and study went on
for some time, the only inconvenience being the necessity
of travelling from Warsaw to Praga and back again every day.
I applied at the personnel department for living quarters
and waited for an answer.

In the meantime I managed to obtain a pass for
Zbyszek. With it, I brought my friend inside the building
complex. I proudly showed him around the place: the massive marble steps leading from the spacious lobby up to the
presidential office, and up again through various ministries
on the floors above.

When we reached the sixth floor, I played host by invit-
ing Zbysezk to lunch at the cafeteria. There, as we ate soup
and cabbage rolls, our conversation turned to music. We discussed the strengths and weaknesses of some of the great-
est composers: Beethoven, Chopin, Tchaikovsky, and others.
So absorbed were we in exchanging our views that we did
not notice the woman who sat next to us, listening to our
conversation. That is, until she spoke.

"Pardon me," she said, "I couldn't help overhearing your
conversation, boys. Tell me, how is it that you are so interested in the great composers?"

I spoke up: "We are both musicians. I study violin at
the conservatory. My name is Arthur and this is Zbyszek."

"My name is Krause," said the woman. She was about
thirty, tall and thin, with brown hair and glasses that
matched the colour of her hair. Her not-unpleasant face had
the sweet and sour expression of an old maid.

"Do you work here? she asked me.

"I do. Zbyszek is a visitor."

"Where do you work and what do you do?" inquired Miss Krause with apparent interest. I was puzzled by her curiosity, but thought that it could do me no harm to answer her questions.

"I work in the Presidium Council of Ministers. I sweep the staircases," I said, looking down at my hands absent-mindedly. A new blister from pushing the broom all day was beginning to form.

Miss Krause followed my gaze. There was a momentary pause. "Does this type of work stiffen your fingers, interfere with your violin technique?" she asked.

"Yes, it does," I answered sadly. I had been noticing some stiffness during my exercises lately.

How would you like to work as a messenger in the Ministry of Culture and Art? I am Minister Rzymowski's secretary. I could arrange it."

"Oh, yes!" I replied eagerly. "I'd like that!"

"Good. I will speak to the director of personnel today and arrange your transfer," said Miss Krause as she wrote down my name and employee number. Zbyszek looked at me with wide-open eyes, having just witnessed my instant promotion. My own facial expression must have matched his. We both laughed.

"Let's skip violin practice today and go to a cinema instead, after I'm through with work," I suggested. Zbyszek agreed.

He had to return to the apartment to run an errand for his mother, but came back and met me at the gates when I got off work. We walked a short block and took our places in a long lineup forming in front of the small run-down building that housed the Lux Cinema. A noisy group of girls in their early teens, ahead of us in line, tried to attract attention to themselves by laughing and shouting. We chose to ignore them and waited impatiently for the line to advance.

After what seemed like a long time, we got close enough to see the glossy photos mounted on faded green material inside the display cases. The photos showed scenes from the movie, which was Russian. Most of the movies in Poland after the war were Russian. The title of this one was *The Secretary of a Region,* and, judging from the scenes in the display out front, it was a war movie. Finally we got in and found seats close to the front of the theatre.

The tale, in Russian with Polish subtitles, unfolded before our eyes. As we watched in suspense, Russian partisan fighters kept harassing the Germans, who had occupied the region, by blowing up bridges and trains.

Then the story became romantic. A pretty, wide-eyed girl who was the radio operator fell in love with a husky blond fellow who looked suspiciously like a German. The girl didn't suspect anything. She was teaching him how to transmit in the Russian code, but he kept making mistakes, which made the girl laugh.

Sure enough, he was a German spy, but the girl didn't suspect anything. She joked about his butterfingers to her superiors, who had been wondering how information about every move was getting to the Germans. After listening to the girl joking, they exchanged knowing looks and started to hum an old Russian melody. In the next scene, the German spy is radioing information about a forthcoming meeting at the town hall while pretending to make love to the girl.

The meeting takes place, but it's the Germans who fall into the trap and are ambushed. In the confusion, the spy escapes. The angry girl chases him to the top of a water tower and shoots him while he begs for mercy. With this happy ending, the movie came to a close, and we left the theatre reassured by the knowledge that, in the end, good always triumphs over evil.

I began my cleaning duties the following morning by picking up my broom and dustpan. I overheard the supervisor complaining about the shortage of rags for cleaning the building, and the high prices he was willing to pay for them due to the scarcity.

An idea flashed through my mind. I recalled having seen a lot of rags scattered among ruins near Zbyszek's apartment. I asked the supervisor, "How much do the rags cost?"

"How much? About 2,000 zlotys for a small bag!" exclaimed the supervisor.

"I could bring you some for 1,000 zlotys a bag."

"Bring them in! We'll pay you 1,000 zlotys a bag!"

I collected all the rags I could find among the ruins on my way to work and was paid for them on delivery. The next morning I heard complaints that the rags disintegrated when they got wet. Fortunately, that was also the day I was to be transferred to the Ministry of Culture and Art, which saved me from having to endure any more criticism of my short-lived rag business.

I was a messenger now, and the Ministry of Culture and Art was on the third floor. The new job, I found, was easy and more pleasant than pushing a broom all day. Most of the time I sat in the ministry's elegantly furnished secretariat waiting for assignments. Miss Krause's massive desk faced the door of Minister Rzymowski's room. Her back was to a wall with large double windows, so there was plenty of natural light. Eight red-plush-upholstered chairs were arranged nearby.

I had a peek at the minister's room, which nearly got me into trouble, as he was there when I appeared in the door. But Rzymowski, a silver-haired man of medium height, only asked who I was. He nodded with a benevolent smile when I told him that I was the new messenger.

My quick peek into the minister's office convinced me that even a Communist regime likes to keep its functionaries in luxurious surroundings. The floor of the room was covered with a magnificent, thick Turkish rug. All the walls were decorated with works of art, almost alive in their elaborate gold frames.

That very same day, I met the director of theatre, Szymanski, when I delivered a letter to him from the director of the department of music, Drobner, whom I immediately recognized as a Jew. Next day brought even more pleasant surprises.

The Frédéric Chopin Conservatory of Music had granted me a stipend of 300 zlotys a month for being an outstanding student. That meant that I did not have to pay for my music lessons. They would pay me for learning, said the principal of the conservatory, Professor Wieniawski.

I was so happy about it that I decided to take piano and accordion lessons, along with my violin lessons. Wieniawski approved of the piano lessons, but his face fell when he heard the word "accordion." He warned me that I would never get a stipend for the accordion lessons. The accordion teacher, he said coolly, was hired solely because of pressure from "certain quarters." He himself, said Wieniawski with disdain, was not in favour of bringing an instrument "such as that," into the conservatory's curriculum.

I listened politely but refused to be dissuaded. I was duly registered for the two additional instruments. The piano and accordion teachers were in the office and overheard the discussion. They introduced themselves to me and commented that my name, Arthur Schaller, would look good on concert posters. I liked hearing that.

I was in a happy mood as I left the conservatory and walked in the warm April sun, my hands in my pockets, whistling a lively tune. My feet felt light, as though they wanted to dance a little jig. As a messenger, my earnings were only slightly better than what I'd gotten as a sweeper, but with the meals at the cafeteria and the food I could buy with my ration card, I could live quite well—that is, without hunger.

The food parcels from the Jewish Committee never materialized, and no one was looking for me yet. The Central Jewish Committee moved from Lublin to a new location in Praga. I went there looking for the kind man who had given me shoes, but he was nowhere to be found.

A week later, I received an answer to my request for new quarters in Praga. I was assigned by the Department of Housing to a small room in a basement apartment, which I was to share with two other boys my age. They too worked for the government. I said good-bye to Zbyszek and his mother, and moved the same day.

The room was part of a hostel, which was run by an enormously fat woman. It had been appropriated, against her bitter protest, by the Department of Housing. After realizing that her complaints were to no avail, she consoled herself by squeezing two more beds into the one room she still controlled. That was her means of earning a living— renting the ten beds in that room by the night to people in transit.

My companions were a good lot. A thin, dark-haired boy named Janek, and a heavyset, red-haired boy named Tadek. They both loved to laugh, and the owner of the hostel became the object of their innumerable jokes, especially Janek's.

I led a busy life. I had three music lessons a week, after work. In order not to disturb the guests in the hostel, I stayed in the Ministry of Culture and Art after everyone had left and practised my violin, playing in the washroom, standing near an open window. Some nights I slept in the typists' room on a small grey couch. I would be wakened by the cleaners in the morning. No one objected—people liked me, and I made many friends.

My small twelve-bass accordion was limiting my progress. The absence of minor and seventh chords restricted me to playing only major keys. I was introduced to a man who had a forty-eight-bass accordion for sale. It was a beautiful pink-pearl-covered accordion with one register. The man wanted 5,000 zlotys for it. My money was almost gone, but I began to look for ways to get the amount I needed to buy the accordion from him.

As a first step, I sold some of my belongings to a street peddler. My German pilot's cap brought in 200 zlotys, a blanket, 600. I sold my food ration for the week, which gave me another 200. I was still 4,000 zlotys short. What to do? I was worried that the accordion would be sold to someone else. I thought about it constantly while running messages from the ministry to other government buildings located throughout Praga and Warsaw. Still, I couldn't come up with a solution to my problem.

Then, when running an errand, I absent-mindedly turned a corner in one of the endless corridors in the government complex and bumped into a boy about my age. He was a messenger for another ministry. As he was heavier than I was, the impact of the collision threw me to the marble floor. Picking myself up, I glanced at the fellow's feet. He was wearing shoes that were identical to the ones I had received from the man at the Central Jewish Committee in Lublin.

First I excused myself and then I asked the boy, "Are you a Jew?" The boy hesitated. I told him that I was a Jew.

"I am too, b-b-but how did you know?" stammered the boy in surprise.

"Your shoes," I explained. The boy looked at my feet and smiled.

"So you got them too," he said.

We started to talk. His name was Jurek. He came from Lublin along with the government some months before. He, too, was alone. His family had been taken away from their village by the Germans. He escaped and was hidden by some farmers who knew his family.

Our conversation continued later. We met at lunch in the cafeteria. As we discussed our jobs and how small our wages were in terms of purchasing value, Jurek said he'd heard that the Central Jewish Committee had money from America specifically designated for loans to Jewish people to help them re-establish themselves.

I became very interested.

"Are you sure?" I eagerly inquired.

"I'm sure," retorted Jurek. "The man who told me about it received a loan."

There was hope now. The same day, right after work, I went to the Central Jewish Committee's office to ask for a loan.

"Have you any sponsors?" asked the man behind the counter.

"Sponsors?" I echoed.

"Yes, sponsors. Two people who will sign for you, guarantee for you. You have to have sponsors to get a loan."

"I will get sponsors," I said with determination.

"Come back when you have them," said the man. He handed me a printed form to be signed by the two sponsors, which I stuck into my pocket. I walked out of the office deep in thought about whom I might ask to sign it.

I walked slowly along Targowa Street and turned the corner to Vilenska Street as my thoughts began to crystallize: I will see Mr. Bebrysz first and then...oh well, we'll see.

Mr. Bebrysz was still at the conservatory when I arrived for my piano lesson. I approached the big man with my heart pounding like a bass drum and presented my problem. The solution was quick. Mr. Bebrysz listened, smiled, and signed!

My piano lesson followed. The piano teacher, knowing that I had no opportunity to practise piano at home, gave me an extra measure of her time, although she never mentioned it. It warmed my heart to see how good most people really are.

That night as I lay on my straw mattress I thought about good and evil. The banter of my roommates, the high-pitched voice of the landlady, and the murmur of the guests in the hostel reached me only faintly. I stared at the ceiling. The irregular patches of peeled-off paint were a lighter shade than the rest of the faded blue ceiling. They looked like clouds, drifting lazily through the sky.

I was in the pastures...I felt a breeze at the back of my neck, and I turned my head to look...

The angel was sitting on a wooden fence, his bare feet skimming the grass below. He held his face in his hands. His large white wings were hanging down behind him. A small herd of cows grazed peacefully in the background. The angel and I looked at each other in silence for a while.

"*Dzien dobry,*" I said.

"*Dzien dobry,*" answered the angel without moving his lips. His voice sounded in my mind, soft and strong. It surprised me to hear the angel speaking Polish. Based on my religious education, I had assumed that Hebrew was the official language of angels, and other heavenly creatures. I heard some voices sounding from afar and wanted to get up and see who was there, but I couldn't move. I looked at the angel again and a feeling of impatience came over me. Why couldn't I get up? And why was the angel here?

"To answer your questions," came the answer. I knew now: I did not have to speak; the angel could hear my thoughts.

"I do have a few questions."

"Ask them then," came the reply.

"Why is there so much evil in this world, if most people are good?

"A single evil one can throw a stone into a well, and ten good ones cannot pull it out."

"Why does God allow him to throw the stone into the well?" I asked with pain, thinking of the Ghetto and of my family, and of all the poor, starving people.

"He doesn't. He gives the good people a lot of time to stop the evil one from throwing the stone. But if they don't stop him, he doesn't interfere. He gave them free will, and the capacity to distinguish between good and evil."

"But how can they stop the evil one without becoming evil themselves?" I asked with desperation, thinking of violence.

"When the evil one is weak, he can be stopped easily," answered the angel. I had nothing more to say after that, and I meditated on the angel's answers, looking up at the sky. The clouds stopped moving and suddenly I was in bed, my hands crossed on my chest, looking at the grey patches on the faded blue ceiling. Janek and Tadek were undressing, talking quietly so as not to wake me.

I closed my eyes and fell into a deep sleep.

The next morning I got up early and went to the ministry. I sat down on one of the red-plush chairs in the secretariat and waited for Miss Krause to come in. I was going to ask her to sign as my second sponsor, but when she arrived I changed my mind. She handed me a letter for Mr. Drobner, director of the Department of Music. He was a man in his forties, of medium height and with carefully combed dark hair. He smiled as I handed him the letter and thanked me. I rubbed the loan form between my fingers, gathering my nerve to speak.

"I am a Jew. I asked for a loan at the Central Jewish Committee, to buy a musical instrument. I need one more sponsor. Perhaps…"

I stopped and handed Mr. Drobner the loan application form. He seemed a bit surprised, but he read it and signed without hesitation. Then he handed it back to me.

"Thank you!" I whispered, as there were other people standing close by.

That very same evening I played my new forty-eight-bass accordion, taking full advantage of the minor and seventh chords. I sold my old accordion the next day.

Several different ways of augmenting my income presented themselves in quick succession. The first one came about when the newspaper vendor who had a small kiosk in the lobby of the government building where I worked approached me with a business proposal. It turned out that he derived most of his income from the sale of cigarettes. He sold Polish and Russian cigarettes openly, but he also sold black-market American cigarettes, which were terribly expensive and very profitable. So profitable, in fact, that he asked me if I could pick up his bundle of newspapers from the distributor every day before noon and bring it to him. He was an old man and it was difficult for him to manage the pick-up. Besides, he had to close his kiosk at prime time and lose out on the cigarette sales.

The distributor's warehouse was not far from the government complex, and working as a messenger I had a fair amount of freedom. So I agreed to do it for 10 zlotys a day.

I took my place in line with crowds of rowdy boys and picked up the bundle of newspapers when my turn came. I did this every working day. On Saturdays, since the government buildings were closed and the vendor's kiosk locked up, I picked up the bundle of newspapers and sold them myself.

On this historically triumphant Saturday in May of 1945, I ran through the streets of Praga joyously shouting: "*Warsaw Courier*! Germany capitulated! Germany capitulated! Get your paper here!"

I sold all my newspapers within minutes. The buyers were so happy about Germany's defeat that they did not even wait for their change.

I found it hard to understand that although Germany had capitulated, the war was not over. Japan was still fighting. I realized as well that for me the war would never be completely over. My losses were too great, and too deep.

But life went on. I kept working, studying, and taking every opportunity to increase my meagre income. I had a loan to pay off. Still, I had mixed feelings about the next source of additional income: packs of American cigarettes stuck into my pockets by total strangers!

It started like this: Miss Krause, besides being the minister's secretary, was busy writing a book. She often left the office for an hour at a time to study and do research for her book at the government library. When she was certain that I could be relied upon and that I knew how to converse with people, she instructed me on answering the secretariat's telephone and on how to decide who should be granted a pass to enter the Ministry of Culture and Art and who shouldn't.

I would receive calls from people who waited at the pass office on Vilenska Street across from the government complex. They gave me their names and stated their reasons for wishing to enter the ministry.

If I thought that the reason was valid, I called the pass office and told them to issue the pass. It made me laugh to think that I had the power to admit a person or refuse entry to the building.

Then it started. Word must have gotten around that I had the authority to issue passes. One day, as I delivered some papers to the pass office, a man followed me and accosted me on the street. He pleaded that I instruct the pass office to issue a pass for him. He said he was a music teacher from another town. It was his third day of trying unsuccessfully to get a pass into the ministry. Before I could stop him, he stuck a package of Camels into my pocket and quickly walked away.

My initial reaction was a feeling of embarrassment, but as my fingers stroked the smooth cellophane, I convinced myself that the man deserved a chance. A little while later, I called the pass office to order a pass for him. The news vendor paid a good price for American cigarettes.

This occurred a couple more times, and I felt worse each time I accepted the cigarettes. Then I made a decision. No more bribes. It was not worth compromising my integrity.

I stuck to my decision and made a habit of keeping both hands in my pockets when I was approached by people on the street.

Then came the opportunity to increase my income in a way that I enjoyed. I was asked to play for a staff party at the Ministry of the Treasury and offered a fee of 500 zlotys for the job. At the party, I found to my surprise that quite independently a pianist had also been engaged. Unfortunately, the tuning of the piano differed from the tuning of my accordion. We took turns playing separately, but the crowd preferred my music to the pianist's, and I ended up playing most of the numbers. I didn't mind that, but I felt sorry for the pianist, who was an unassuming older man.

Following the success of this party came an invitation to perform at another, this one organized by the secret police. I took along my old partner, Zbyszek, and split the fee of 800 zlotys with him. Even at their party, the secret police carried heavy handguns in leather holsters, the handles protruding menacingly and swaying as they danced. It reminded me in a macabre way of some of the American cowboy pictures I had seen at Saturday matinees before the war, when I was seven or eight.

About three-quarters of the faces of the men and women attending the Ministry of Security party looked Jewish, but not the kind of gentle Jewish faces I had grown up among. The eyes of these men and women—especially the men—were hard and untrusting. They would not smile, no matter how much we tried to make them happy with our music.

Still, they liked our performance and the popular songs we played, and told us so at the end of the party.

One day I received a pass to attend a concert given by the famous Russian violinist, Miss Maslova. It was very funny—not the concert; she played beautifully. It was my sitting in the first row with all the important people behind me. You see, the ticket was really meant for Minister Rzymowski, who could not attend and gave the ticket to Miss Krause, who could not attend either and then passed the ticket on to me. That's how I ended up in the minister's seat.

And so, quite apart from the enjoyment of listening to a violin virtuoso, I had a lot of fun observing the expressions on people's faces when I looked back during the intermission.

On another night, after performing at a government-sponsored event, I was invited by some young people to a party just across from the government complex. There I met Lydia. She and I were drawn to one another and eventually decided to leave the party in search of privacy. Hand in hand, we ventured out into the rainy night. I carried my accordion across my back, my coat draped over it. We ran across the street and showed our passes to the soldiers on guard. Once in the typists' room, I pulled three chairs over to the couch to make a bed for myself, and she lay on the couch. She left at sunrise.

That was my introduction to lovemaking. Now I knew that I was capable of giving pleasure to a woman. I was seventeen years old, and she was about twenty-five. It was not love, of course. It took me many more years and more sexual encounters to learn what love is and what it is not.

We saw each other just once after that night, in one of the marble halls filled with passersby. She turned her head towards me several times, expecting me to speak. I could not bring myself to say or do anything. Shortly after that, I left Warsaw and never saw her again.

I thought about my family often, trying to re-create each face, each image of a whole living person pulled gently from the recesses of my memory. Sometimes I pressed both hands against my temples, desperately willing my reluctant eyes to give up the reality of here and now and project visions of people and places that were no more. I filled the rooms with images of dimly remembered uncles, aunts, and cousins who moved and laughed and talked.

My memories of family usually revolved around Sabbath visits. My parents and I were invited from time to time to partake in *cholent* and *kugel* midday meals. These aromatic meals were prepared overnight in bakery ovens and picked up after services. The commandment to keep the Sabbath as a day of rest forbade cooking on Saturday.

We ate the delectable blend of brown baked potatoes, beef chunks, barley, and beans, which had been sealed in large paper-covered *cholent* pots. In a smaller pot enclosed within it nestled the golden *kugel*, a pudding made of noodles and raisins. The discussions after the meal, accompanied by a glass of sweet raisin wine (of which I was permitted a sip or two), were always lively and spirited.

One of my mother's two brothers lived on Ceglana Street, the other on Zamenhofa Street. The bitter irony of my failing memory was that I could not for the life of me remember their first names. Their family names were of course my mother's maiden name, Glaschmit, but there were blank spaces where my uncles' names should have been.

The faces of my mother and father dimmed and lost their sharpness. I had no photos of them to remind me precisely how they looked. All I had left were my feelings and the memories of places within which my family had once lived and moved. I did have a small photo of my brother. Thank God, I would be able to remember his face.

Another pass, a permanent one entitling its holder to two seats in any movie theatre, was circulated among the employees of the ministry. Eventually my turn came, and I invited Zbyszek to see a Russian movie called *Stalingrad*. It showed the tide of battle turning against the Germans. Stalingrad marked the beginning of their defeat, and they hadn't ceased retreating since their defeat there. We enjoyed watching the movie in spite of the usual hefty dose of propaganda.

Speaking of propaganda, I remember the day a soldier in a Russian uniform sat down on a park bench beside me while I ate my lunch. It was a tiny park not far from the government complex. The soldier struck up a conversation and began praising the quality of life in Russia.

According to him, people living in the Soviet Union had everything their hearts desired. I knew better. I had spoken with other soldiers and civilians who had been there, and the stories they told were quite different. However, I did not argue with him but pretended to agree with everything he said. The soldier left very pleased, and I never saw him again.

The surprising part of it came when Janek told me that he had the same experience the following day. According to Janek's description of him, it was the very same soldier asking the same questions and telling the same stories. Clearly, we were being tested for our political opinions, especially what we thought about the Soviet Union.

Just about that time, application forms were being handed out to all ministry employees for the Government Workers' Union. This created an atmosphere of great fear and agitation among the workers, who suspected that they were being coerced into becoming members of the Communist Party, and no one wanted that. Finally, they were convinced that it was only a workers' association. Some joined and some did not. I didn't join. I was too busy with my music lessons to bother with labour movements.

One day after work I played my accordion while Janek and Tadek listened, making occasional requests. I sat on my bed since there were no chairs in our little room.

A diminutive Russian officer walked in. He was tightly built, short and slim. His uniform insignia and shoulder ornaments were that of a captain, with a leather belt and shoulder stripe over his shirt jacket. He flashed a wide, friendly grin as he leaned against the wall, listening to the accordion. I was used to visitors from the adjacent hostel when I played, but I had never seen a uniformed officer of the Red Army here before.

He could have been anywhere between thirty and forty and had brown eyes and a tightly drawn face, with lines running straight from cheek to chin. He reminded me of a humorous little devil when he laughed, revealing small pointed teeth.

"*Harasho! Harasho! Ochen harasho!* Good! Good! Very good!" he exclaimed in Russian, clapping his hands enthusiastically as I finished my number. I could not resist liking him, and smiled back appreciatively. He came closer and stretched out his hand in a hearty gesture.

"My name is Misha Bukoviecki! I, too, am an artist." He paused for a moment in order to allow the importance of his words to sink in. Before I had an opportunity to inquire about the nature of his artistry, he announced proudly: "I am The Man Made of Rubber!" He elaborated: "I do acrobatics and perform magic tricks. I am a Red Army veteran and have many decorations!"

While he spoke, he pumped my hand with his own small yet very strong hand.

"I am very pleased to know you," I said. I was fascinated by this quick, clever man.

"Can you play Strauss waltzes?" asked Misha.

I could. I played the "Blue Danube" waltz for him. He liked it and asked for more. I played the "Emperor" waltz, the "Vienna Blut," and "Tales from the Vienna Woods" for him. This took quite a bit of time, since Strauss waltzes are rather lengthy. By the time I finished playing my last waltz, my roommates had gone outside to the street to get some fresh air.

Misha made a proposal: "I need a musician to play Strauss waltzes while I perform on stage," he said. "I will pay you after each performance. What you get will depend on how many tickets we sell, but I will pay you well. Good?"

"Good," I agreed, and the deal was made.

A few days went by, and I only saw Misha once, and very briefly at that. He introduced me to his wife, a pale, thin woman from Holland. She and Misha occupied one of the beds in the hostel. In the bed next to theirs to the right was an old man from Cracow, and in a bed on their left side slept a green-uniformed policewoman from Lodz.

Beds were rented without any regard to privacy between the sexes. This was a difficult period of time. Most of Warsaw's buildings had been destroyed, and more and more people were flooding into the city, increasing the shortage of accommodations. One Sunday morning I had the good fortune of gaining access to the one washroom shared by all the inhabitants of the hostel. As I washed my hands and face, Misha came in and announced, "Arthur, today we give a concert for the Polish soldiers."

"Good!" I said. "What time does it start?"

"In the afternoon," said Misha. "About three o'clock."

The hall was small and crowded with Polish soldiers. In fact, it wasn't a hall at all. It was the living room of a ground-floor apartment. There were few chairs, and everyone was just standing around, talking and laughing. Misha's wife was selling tickets at the door. She too was standing, holding a roll of pink tickets in one hand and a crumpled bundle of zlotys in the other.

The soldiers were looking at Misha now. He was the only one in the room wearing a Russian uniform with the shiny insignia of an officer on his shoulders. He pocketed the money and suddenly clapped his hands.

"Comrades!" he shouted. "The show is about to begin! I, Misha Bukoviecki, The Man Made of Rubber, will show you first...a few of my acrobatic acts!" He pointed his index finger at me. "Accordionist! Play Strauss!"

I was taken by surprise. Quickly, I put on the accordion straps and started to play the "Blue Danube." The audience moved back to make room for Misha, who spread his arms, indicating to the soldiers how much room he needed. Then he did a few back flips, a quick handstand, and bowed for applause.

"Thank you! Thank you! Would someone hand me a chair, please?" A chair was passed to him over the soldiers' heads. Misha placed it in front of him and did a handstand on it. Then he jumped down to the floor, still on his hands, and walked around in a circle. Still standing on his hands, Misha bowed to acknowledge the audience's applause. Then he did a back flip and landed on his feet again. His compact body, like a coiled spring, moved with cat-like smoothness and self-assured fluidity. I kept playing until Misha gave me a hand signal to stop.

"And now! I will perform for you…a few magic tricks! Does anyone own a watch? A good watch? One that works?"

A few soldiers held out their watches. Misha chose a watch and, with an exaggerated gesture, lifted it above his head. Turning slowly in a full circle, he showed it to the whole audience. Then he produced a box made of multi-coloured cardboard with a pullout drawer into which the soldier's watch disappeared. Misha then made a number of wavy motions over the box.

"Now! Let us see this fine watch!" he intoned. With these words, he opened the drawer and lifted out a toy watch made of tin, which he handed to the owner to the accompaniment of laughter from the audience. Of course, everyone had figured out that the box had a trick compartment. Still, I could see that the soldier was worried about getting his watch back. A moment later, however, with a magical pass of his hand, Misha changed the toy watch back into the original. Then the soldier who owned the watch was laughing as well.

I played another waltz while Misha performed a few card tricks, and the show was over. The soldiers filed out through the door. Misha was pleased.

"It was a good show and you played well," he told me with a grin. "But the next time we'll have a larger hall," he announced as he counted out 50 zlotys into my hand, which seemed fair for a half-hour's work. Then Misha's wife approached us and took him to the side. She started to argue with him, speaking German. Misha responded in what I at first thought was broken German—then recognized as Yiddish!

Misha was a Jew! I realized with a shock. His wife was definitely not Jewish. They argued about broken promises of some kind, and I left quickly so as not to overhear a family argument.

The following few days were uneventful. I did my routine work at the ministry, attended my music lessons at the conservatory, and practised during most of my spare time. Then one day, while delivering an open letter to the director of the department of music, I noticed Mr. Bebrysz's name in the heading. It was a complaint from a music teacher about Mr. Bebrysz, who was assistant director of the conservatory. The letter stated that Mr. Bebrysz had failed to pay the teacher's wages on time, and it listed other complaints as well, all against Mr. Bebrysz.

I was concerned about Mr. Bebrysz. I knew that he was a good man. I also had an obligation, as a messenger, to deliver the letter, and I did so. But right after work I went to see Mr. Bebrysz and cautioned him about the complaint.

Mr. Bebrysz listened, then laughed. "The man is a troublemaker," he said. "Nothing to worry about." He thanked me for my concern, and he commented with some wonderment on how things had changed for me. Why, only a few months ago, I was standing at his doorway, trying to sell him my violin! And now I was able to help him. We shook hands and parted. I was glad that the threat to him was not serious, and only felt a little guilty for giving away a matter that was confidential in an attempt to save a friend.

Misha did rent a larger hall for the next show, which took place the following Sunday. It was a movie theatre with a narrow stage. The audience consisted mostly of civilians, who occupied only about a third of the available seats. I was the only musician in a spacious orchestra pit. I tried hard to make up in volume for being a one-man band. Misha went through his act in front of the white movie screen, framed by a purple curtain.

The applause was as brief and lukewarm as an April shower. The show lasted about forty-five minutes and, when it was over, Misha gave me 70 zlotys and said, "You did a good job. I'm going to organize a theatrical troupe with you as my musician."

I walked out of the theatre with my accordion slung over my shoulder by the straps. Praga's sidewalks basked in warm sunlight and the air smelled good. The chestnut trees lining the sidewalks were old, massive, and laden with leaves. Summer was palpable in Praga. It was different in the ruins of Warsaw itself. The ever-present acrid smell of the rubble made it almost impervious to the changes of the seasons.

I was overcome by feelings of sadness and loneliness that Sunday afternoon after the performance. I had been running away from them by keeping busy and setting goals for myself. But loneliness had caught up with me now. The absence of my loved ones was like a wound that would not heal. Every inquiry about my family at the office of the Jewish Committee was more painful than the last because it seemed to confirm what I had known all along: I was alone. There was no one left alive of all my family. No one except possibly my father—my father, somewhere in Russia. I held on to this hope with all my strength and against all my doubts.

On reaching the hostel, I descended the four steps at the entrance and greeted the owner, then went to my room and gently removed the accordion from my shoulder. Placing it on the bed, I lay down beside it and pressed my cheek to the rough blanket.

I heard Misha and his wife arguing as they entered the hostel. Then there was a moment of silence, followed by a scream. I jumped off the bed, and just then Misha came running into the room shouting, "Arthur! Get a doctor! She took poison! That stupid woman! Go quickly! She might die!"

I ran out the door and kept running until I found a doctor. I took him to the hostel, then went to my room and waited. The hostel owner came into my room. Her face bore an unusually tender expression. She pressed her hands together in a gesture of compassion and shook her head several times. "Poor thing, she's been like this ever since she lost her baby. I know what that means. I lost three of them, and then my husband died. He will have to watch out. She took some pills. I don't know where she got them."

I listened with a new understanding of how little one really knows about people until their hearts speak out. I knew that I would never again laugh at my roommates' jokes about this woman.

"Is she going to be all right?"

"Yes," she replied. "He took away the box before she could swallow too many. But he'd better watch her or next time…" She gestured helplessly and left the room.

For several days following the suicide attempt, I didn't see Misha or his wife. Then, on Thursday, Misha was waiting for me in front of the hostel when I got home from work. There was a big grin on his face, and I knew that he had some good news.

"My friend," he said, accosting me grandly, taking me by the elbow and steering me along the street. "I have assembled a whole troupe—bicyclists, dancers, acrobats—everything! We are going to tour Russia! And you are going with us! Just like I promised. Well! How do you like that?"

My heart was beating fast. This was the first time Misha had mentioned a tour of Russia. All he'd said before was that he wanted to organize a troupe. Still, here was a chance to look for my father. My only chance, perhaps. Yet it was not a decision to be taken lightly—to leave my job, the conservatory lessons, my room in the hostel, and to go into the huge, unknown country of Russia with nothing but hope.

"I will go with you," I heard myself say, as if my voice emanated from elsewhere.

"Good!" exclaimed Misha joyfully. "I will show you Mother Russia, and we will make money too—lots of money!"

"When are we leaving?" I asked, still in a daze.

"Tomorrow morning! Everything is arranged! A truck is

coming to pick us up! The rest of the troupe will be on it!"

"Tomorrow morning? So soon? Things are really moving fast!"

"Yes, we already have a hall rented in Kielce for our first performance!" announced Misha confidently. He left to make arrangements for the following day.

I went back to the hostel to pack my things. My sudden move surprised my roommates less than I expected. I gave each of them some odds and ends of my wardrobe. One of my rubber boots had a hole in it, so I gave them to Janek. Tadek inherited a couple of my older shirts and a German knapsack. The rest of my "war surplus" went to the hostel owner. Everyone wished me success in my new venture. They didn't know about my father. I had never told anyone. They considered my journey to be simply the first step in an exciting musical career.

The truck arrived at about ten the next morning. There had been some delay in picking up the other performers. Misha and his wife went into the driver's cab, and I sat down on a wooden bench inside the canvas-covered rear of the truck, stuffing my two bags under the bench. The truck was so fully loaded with equipment and filled with people that I had to hold my accordion on my knees. The engine roared, and the truck began to move.

With the ties of my recent life now cleanly severed, I started to give myself over to the new experience. I looked around, observing the faces of my travelling companions. There was a short, muscular man, about twenty-five, who kept throwing his head back, trying to keep his straight, dark hair out of his eyes while talking to his wife. She was short and dark haired as well, and wore more makeup than most Polish women.

Next to them sat a somewhat older woman in a flowered blouse. She was part of the bicycle acrobat trio. One of the two men she was with, a blond heavyset man, propped two shiny bikes up against the truck canvas to prevent them from moving. He was most likely her husband. The other man, also blond and with a short, stubby nose, was younger and slimmer than his partner. I knew that they belonged together because the two men wore identical light blue costumes with dark blue stripes.

There was another couple, older then the rest. The man's hair was thinning on top, and he wore shiny oversized dentures. He was heavyset and of medium height. His companion was a slight woman about his age, a brunette with a serious face and worried green eyes. She looked at me and at my accordion, and smiled. I nodded in greeting and then looked away to the passing streets of Praga visible through the rear gate of the truck.

My past was rolling away before my eyes. My future was as blank as when I had left the Warsaw Ghetto, in August of 1942. Only less, yes, much less dangerous, I reassured myself.

The town of Kielce lies about 140 kilometres south of Warsaw. It is the main town in a district bearing the same name. The major cities closest to it are Cracow and

Katowice, which lie about a hundred kilometres farther south, towards the Czechoslovakian border.

I remembered these facts from my geography lessons at school. I knew that one could travel from one end of Poland to the other in this direction and still keep approximately the same distance from the Russian border.

The "concerts," as Misha called them, were performed in the largest hall in Kielce. We gave three concerts of less then mediocre quality, really a sprinkling of poor circus acts without animals.

The hall was filled to capacity during our first two performances. It seemed that the audience was starved for any kind of entertainment. However, as word of mouth got around, the hall was only half filled during the third and last performance in Kielce.

But as far as the members of Misha Bukoviecki's troupe were concerned, the money was good and they had no intention of going to Russia, and, as they put it, "working for the government." They decided instead to continue touring Poland and making bundles of money. That part of Misha's prediction turned out to be true—for them, that is. Not for me. I was not interested in money, not now. I wanted to find my father.

I complained bitterly to Misha. "Is this why I left the ministry and the conservatory? To wander around Poland with a circus? Why didn't you tell me we weren't going to Russia after all? I would never have left Warsaw."

Misha tried to laugh it off. He attempted to convince

me that making money was not be scorned. Wasn't it important? Not to me. Not any more. I longed for a sense of identity, of belonging. I could not identify with this troupe. I did not belong here. Against the protests of Misha and other members of the troupe, I decided to quit. They left with a local accordion player, someone they found at the last minute to replace me.

I could not go back to Warsaw. I had left my job at the ministry without giving notice. My job was surely lost, I reflected, as I woefully examined my now-useless entry pass into the government buildings.

There were expenses to be met. After I paid the weekly rent for my room and bought some food, I nearly exhausted my meagre resources. A roomer in the apartment next door sold me four cartons of matches, which were in short supply at the time. I sold them by the box at the local marketplace. That kept me from going hungry for the next two days, after which I walked into a market restaurant, carrying my accordion on my shoulder.

I approached the owner, suggesting that his business might improve if he provided music for his customers. The restaurateur agreed, but he refused to spend any money for the entertainment. Instead, he offered to provide two meals a day for my service. In addition, I could keep all tips offered by the customers. I had little choice but to accept the offer. I was hungry. And so, for the next seven days I played at the restaurant, receiving tips for special requests and leading a day-to-day existence. After a week I contacted another restaurant owner on the town's main street and made a better agreement: for playing four hours a day, I received a small sum of money plus one meal daily, and I was allowed to keep all tips. The one drawback of the new job was an old gramophone, which blared hits from the past during my breaks.

One afternoon I felt more than usually irritated by the senseless blaring of the gramophone. The songs were old, worn, and syrupy-sentimental. Also, the needle was dull and the distortion was hurting my ears. Unfortunately, the restaurant owner liked them, and loved to hear them full volume.

A Polish soldier walked in and sat down at a table near me. I was holding my accordion on my knees, enduring the cacophony of the gramophone. The restaurateur walked over to take his order. To my great satisfaction, the first thing the soldier asked was to have the blasted thing turned off. Next, he invited me to join him at his table and ordered food and drinks for both of us.

Sitting across from him, I studied my benefactor's appearance. It seemed to me that there was something familiar and sympathetic about the man. He wasn't young, perhaps forty. His complexion, hair, and eyes were dark, and he had a kind face. He wore no insignia of rank.

"Would you play something for me?" the soldier asked with a smile.

"What would you like to hear?" I replied.

"Do you know '*Bei Mir Bistdu Sheyn*'?"

"Yes," I said, and played it for him. It was a Jewish song,

but sung by others as well. Could he be? But he didn't say. I played some Russian and Polish songs after that, and we ate and drank together. After a couple glasses of vodka, I mustered enough courage to ask him a personal question. I hesitated...

"Are you, by any chance, a Jew?"

"I am," he concurred. "Are you?".

I nodded. "Yes, I am. I didn't know there were any Jews in Kielce."

"There are. They all live in one house at number 7 Planty." The soldier left after a while, sticking a 20-zloty note into my pocket as he got up.

When my work was over, I slung my accordion on my shoulder and left the restaurant, walking down the main street towards the address the soldier had mentioned. The "Jewish house" turned out to be quite close. To think that it had been here all this time, and I hadn't been aware that it existed!

It was a warm summer evening. Soft breezes caressed my brow with velvet fingers. I drank in the cool air as if it were a precious elixir. The noises of a small town past sundown were pleasant—quiet laughter, a child talking to himself, a mother singing a lullaby. My rubber-soled shoes made almost no sound on the sidewalk. For a moment I felt the rapture of my soul making contact and mingling with the spirits of the rest of humanity, saying, Look, here I am. I am one of you. Without the weight of pride, greed, and hate, we are all one, children of God. And we can all communicate, and love, and share the infinite beauty of the universe.

I stopped and looked up to the sky—sending my soul on a journey into the starry space. It travelled for a while, admiring the hugeness, amusing itself with the twinkling lights and gathering respect, awe, and veneration for its Creator. But the farther it went, the colder it got, and it came back to Earth, saying, Here I belong, with the rest of humanity. And it warmed itself again by participating in humanity's presence.

I resumed my walk, knowing that I had found something of myself during my soul's brief journey.

Kibbutz Ihud was on the fourth floor of 7 Planty Street, right at the top of the building. The floors below were occupied by Jewish families. A man I met downstairs, seeing that I was alone and that I was young and looking for other Jews, directed me to the kibbutz upstairs.

I knew that a kibbutz in Poland meant a group of young people preparing themselves for the journey to Palestine. My heart was beating in expectation as I climbed the three flights of concrete steps. I heard laughter and singing even before I reached the door, and the shuffling of dancing feet. The song was Hebrew, powerful and joyous. I didn't recognize this particular song, although I'd learned quite a few Hebrew songs when I was a member of the Faiwuszyc Choir and Hashomer Hatzair in the Ghetto. The dance sounded like a hora. After a few minutes of listening, I recognized the title of the song since it was repeated many times:

"*Adamah*"—meaning Earth, the land of Palestine, the Promised Land.

I opened the door and walked into a large room. After closing the door behind me, I stood there transfixed, watching the young people dancing the hora. Their arms joined together, they formed a circle and sang as they danced. Others, some younger, some older, stood around them and sang and clapped their hands to the driving rhythm. Their eyes shone brightly, reflecting the light of the Sabbath candles, which, in a silvery candelabra dominated the scene from a table covered with a white cloth by the far wall. The dancers picked up speed. The singing stopped and only the six-count stamping of their feet was heard. Then someone began to sing another hora song, one that I knew.

Slowly I slid the accordion off my shoulder, put it on, opened the locking strap, and started to play.

Soon the singing stopped and only the sound of the dancers' feet and my music could be heard. Everyone in the room looked at me, at first with surprise, then with ever-brighter, smiling eyes.

They started to clap again, but did not sing so as to hear me better. A man who was older than the rest, with dark hair and dark, burning eyes, came over to me and put his hand on my shoulder, gently leading me to the centre of the dancers' circle. The circle opened for a moment to let me in.

I stood there and played and played, while the bright faces—young bodies swaying in unison—twirled around me.

I put everything I had into the music. My head was spinning, as I watched the human kaleidoscope. I was happy! Happy for the first time in years!

At last, some of the dancers couldn't catch their breath. They started to drop out of the circle, while the remaining ones closed the temporary gaps with their entwined arms and continued dancing. Finally only five remained, all boys, and they too stopped in the end. They received an enthusiastic round of applause, and so did I.

During the next half-hour I was busy asking and answering questions, talking to many of the boys and girls who came over to me and were eager to know who I was and where I had come from. Someone pulled over a chair for me. They in turn told me all about the kibbutz.

The name of it, Ihud, was the Hebrew word for "unity." At the end of the war, all the Zionist organizations in Poland had dropped their political differences. This kibbutz was formed after the war. Right now, only Zion was important to them—and going to the land of Israel, at any cost, to build a new life. (There were many political differences in Zionist organizations before the war, from extreme left to extreme right.)

All the young people I spoke with were survivors like me. Some of them survived the German concentration camps. Some came out of hiding at the end of the war. Many of them had lost their families and had no one except their new-found friends in Kibbutz Ihud. Tonight they celebrated the Oneg Shabbat, (Celebration of

Sabbath,) which, according to Jewish tradition, begins on Friday at sundown.

The man who had led me into the circle during the dancing came over and greeted me warmly. "*Shalom*," he said, "you have beautified our Oneg Shabbat. We haven't heard Hebrew songs played for a long time. Please, sit down at the table and have something to eat and drink. My name is Hillel."

I accepted the invitation and, while I ate, conversed with Hillel, who turned out to be the leader of the kibbutz. He told me how the kibbutz had been established just three months earlier. There were kibbutzim like this one in cities throughout Poland, where groups of young people, survivors of the German occupation, came together with one idea in mind: to leave the blood-soaked earth of Poland and—for their own sake, for the sake of their children, and for the sake of all the people of Israel—to settle in Palestine. To plant their own vineyards, speak their own language, be free and strong and not subject to the whims of tyrants and madmen. Not to be used as scapegoats by misguided religionists who preach hatred in the name of love. To heal their wounds and fulfil the Bible's prophecy of being the light to all nations.

Hillel's eyes were shining with love for his people as he spoke. "Join us," he said, "Come with us to Eretz Israel, the Land of Israel."

It didn't take me long to make up my mind. That was what my soul yearned for—a feeling of belonging, a sense of identity, an aim in life. I joined the kibbutz.

That night, I slept in a kibbutz bed, and the next morning I got up early and ate my breakfast at a long table with my new friends. Members of the group took turns serving the meals, and I was told that my turn would come next week. The food was simple but good and served in sufficient quantity. To supplement the food rations provided by the Central Jewish Committee, some members of the kibbutz worked at various jobs in the city and contributed all of their earnings to the kibbutz treasury.

Members of the kibbutz were allowed to keep private property. Food and laundry, however, were provided by the kibbutz and one could ask for money if it was needed. I received enough money from the treasurer to pay off the overdue rent at the rooming house where I'd been living. I went there early, shortly after breakfast, and picked up my belongings.

The decision was made. I was now a member of Kibbutz Ihud, waiting impatiently for my journey to the Promised Land.

The group numbered forty teenagers—seventeen girls and twenty-three boys, as well as Hillel and his wife. The boys had two rooms for themselves, and the girls had one large one. There also was a dining room, a kitchen, and a very tiny room, which was more like a large closet. Hillel and his wife slept there, and it served as Hillel's office as well. Three-level bunk beds made it possible to accommodate forty-two people in a six-room apartment.

Since I was the twenty-fourth boy in the group, my

presence brought balance to the distribution of boys in their two rooms. Now there were twelve of us in each room.

I was assigned an upper berth. It took a bit of getting used to, sleeping so close to the ceiling! The ventilation was good, though, because the windows were kept open at all times.

The boys were a good bunch, some of them quite simple, some very intelligent, all of them unassuming, and each in his own way appreciative and good-natured. My bunk mates, Calek and Mordecai, in that order down, were as different from each other as fish from foul. They kidded each other at every opportunity, and yet one could see that they were the best of friends. Calek was fat, with a wide face, blue eyes, and straight brown hair. He moved slowly and was a slow thinker—but he was very consistent once he had reached a decision. Mordecai was thin, with unruly dark blond hair and blue eyes. His mind was as unruly as his hair. He was quick in quoting facts, answering questions, or replying to quips. But he lacked the cement to combine his wit into a creative wholeness. Calek provided the cement, and thus they balanced each other splendidly.

The girls formed their own unit. The group mixed during the activities, lessons, and recreation. But there were no romances blooming as yet, and the girls led a life quite their own, just as the boys did. Hillel's wife, Rosie, acted as sort of a matron over them.

Rules of morality and propriety were strictly enforced. Once it was discovered that two girls, Miriam and Esther, had cuddled together in one bunk and kissed each other on the neck, leaving tell-tale bluish marks. They were scolded in strong terms by Rosie and moved to different bunks, away from each other. It was the only incident of this sort I can remember.

My days were filled with activity. I continued playing in the restaurant on the main street, contributing all my earnings to the kibbutz treasury. I was learning Hebrew and Jewish history and taking part in gymnastics, as well as performing my duties at the tables and in the kitchen. Of course, since I was the kibbutz's only musician, I took part in every singing and dancing session. I played many new songs, which I learned during these sessions. In fact, that's what I liked best, playing for the group. Everything was transformed when they sang the Hebrew songs. The crowded apartment became an open camp under the stars, with a lively campfire in the centre. The group of young survivors, some of whom had gone through untold tortures during the war, became pioneers in their own free land, Israel. That's what I saw and felt when I played for them, and this vision was stronger than the reality of the crowded apartment.

Two months had passed since I had joined the kibbutz, and I felt quite at home. I had little time to think about the past during the day. It was different at night. Sometimes I would lie on my bunk for hours, unable to sleep—thinking of my family and my childhood. Sometimes I relived whole scenes from my childhood and cried when emptiness again engulfed visions of the past.

The soldier who gave me the address of the kibbutz came to visit us during the High Holidays of Rosh Hashanah (New Year's) and Yom Kippur (Day of Atonement). He prayed with the others in the living room, which we converted to a *shul* for these occasions. He was happy to find me in the kibbutz. Some of the families from the lower floors came to visit us and invariably brought the nostalgia of the past with them. Being older, they remembered more of the good things.

During the part of the service when a prayer is said for the dead, tears came uncontrollably to my eyes. I did not have to hide them. There was not one person in the room who wasn't mourning his or her dead.

After the holidays, everyone worked and played harder than ever before, and a feeling of purification and dedication to building a better future swept through the kibbutz. We looked forward to being in Eretz Israel. We knew that when we arrived there, we would have to work even harder, get used to a different climate, and turn a scorched desert into a blooming garden with our bare hands. That would be a labour of love, born of desperation and moulded by an unyielding hope for our future.

We learned that after our arrival in Israel, we would stay for a while in an established kibbutz. After the training period, the Jewish authorities would give us as much land as we could handle—most likely in an unsettled region. We would also receive a loan to carry us through to the first harvest. We would receive some farming equipment too, perhaps some livestock. The rest was up to us.

After we became self-sufficient, we would repay the loan and continue building, planting, and improving the farm. A prosperous kibbutz can provide a good living for its members, and even higher education for children who show an aptitude for learning.

At the same time, the pioneers would be building the Jewish land, redeeming the soil from centuries of barrenness. We would also be paving the way for other victims of oppression who were seeking the opportunity to take part in the rebuilding of their land. Could there be a higher aim for someone whose whole family had been slaughtered because they were Jews?

My opportunity to start the journey came unexpectedly. The kibbutz in Cracow was ten people short of the usual number for crossing the border of Poland. They requested that ten members of our kibbutz be transferred to their kibbutz in order to fill the quota. The moment I heard the news, I ran to Hillel and asked to be included in the transfer—to be one of the ten to go to Cracow.

Hillel was reluctant to let me go. My accordion playing helped to maintain good morale. Also, my earnings from the restaurant were a welcome addition to the treasury of the kibbutz, small as they were.

But I was unyielding in my desire to start my journey to Eretz Israel. I begged. I threatened to leave the kibbutz. I didn't let go until, finally, Hillel gave in. In the end he promised that I would be among those transferred to Cracow.

Two days later I was boarding the train along with five other boys and four girls from my kibbutz. Calek and Mordecai were also among the lucky ten. A man from the Cracow kibbutz accompanied us.

I was so excited about this new adventure that I hardly noticed anything during our train ride. It was only after we arrived in Cracow that I began to look around and observe the sights of the ancient city. It was beautiful, without a doubt, but my interest in it was fleeting. After all, I was on my way to Israel.

The building housing the Cracow kibbutz was old and dilapidated. Inside was a beehive of activity. Everyone was packing and shouting, running to and fro. The fresh faces of my new companions passed before me with a quick "*Shalom!*" and disappeared before I had time to acknowledge the greetings. I met them later at lunchtime in the kibbutz dining room and I liked every one of them.

Shortly after lunch a list of names was read out, and everyone lined up and listened to the instructions given by the man in charge.

"Listen carefully," he said. "You are on the first step of your journey to Eretz Israel. It is not an easy journey. There are many borders to cross, many difficulties to overcome. Some of them have been taken care of by those who paved the way for you. Other challenges you will have to handle— every one of you—as they come.

"First, you will board a train to Katowice. I want you to use common sense, to attract as little attention as possible on that train, which will take you to a town at the border with Czechoslovakia. You will stay together on that train. Things have been arranged for you. Then, as you disembark from the train you will approach the border checkpoint and have your things examined by the Polish border guards.

"Now, here comes the important thing to remember: you are leaving Poland as displaced Greeks! That, too, has been arranged. Remember! Not a word of Polish is to be spoken to the border guards. How to go about it, I will leave to your own ingenuity. Remember, you are leaving Poland as Greeks—it's the only way. Legally, the border is closed to all Polish citizens, which you still are.

"Another thing...all papers, documents, and photographs—anything at all that could identify you as Polish citizens—must be handed over to me now.

"Good luck! May we all meet in Eretz Israel!"

We arrived at the border of Czechoslovakia. The same train was to take us into Czechoslovakia after we had been searched by the border guards. We disembarked and lined up in front of two wooden shacks.

It was late evening. The darkness was broken by a few bare electric bulbs hanging between the shacks and by the headlights of the hissing locomotive waiting nearby.

A thin rain was falling in warm droplets, washing our faces, taking the place of tears.

"Isn't he one of our boys?" wondered one of the Polish guards, speaking to his colleague as they both searched my belongings.

"He *does* look like one of our boys," agreed the guard, looking at me with narrowing eyes.

It was my turn to act. I pronounced the morning prayer in Hebrew, making it sound as if I was talking to them, trying to carry on a conversation, asking about something:

"*Moideh ani lifonechah melech chai v'kayoim*"

"Nah. He couldn't be one of our boys," said the guard. "He speaks Greek." They let me pass after confiscating a pair of new socks from my bundle.

"No new things can be taken out of Poland," one guard explained to me, talking slowly as if speaking to a foreigner. I let out another litany of prayers.

This time, the Four Questions of Passover. And that is how I crossed the border, saying, "*Ma nishtanah halailah ha'ze mikol haleilois?*" (Why is this night different from all other nights?)

# postscript

—

I NEVER SAW MY MOTHER AGAIN AFTER SHE WAS TAKEN from the Ghetto in July of 1942. I do not know when, where, or how she died. The rest of my family in the Warsaw Ghetto, including my brother, Jerzyk, perished during the uprising in the spring of 1943. My father died in Uzbekistan or Kazakhstan during an epidemic.

Six months after I left Kibbutz Ihud in Kielce to join the group in Crakow that was leaving for Israel, there was a pogrom in Kielce. On July 4, 1946, a mob attacked, killing forty-two Jewish men, women, and children and wounding about fifty more. All of the victims were survivors of the Holocaust. Seven men were found guilty and hanged. After the Kielce pogrom, there was a mass exodus of 100,000 Polish Jews who, for the most part, would otherwise have stayed in Poland.

---

To continue where the memoir ends: after crossing snowy fields into Czechoslovakia, our group from the Crakow kibbutz took the train to Carlsbad, where we entered Germany. Our destination was a kibbutz in Deggendorf. I remember our arrival at the kibbutz, the sight of children eating buns with Swiss cheese and drinking cocoa. I hadn't seen such delicious-looking food in years.

In July 1946, reactions to the Kielce pogrom split the Zionist movement into political factions. I had become active in the Yiddish theatre, first with the Naj Theatre in Deggendorf. In August, I joined Theatre Menorah and travelled across Germany, first to Bergen-Belsen, which had become a DP camp. One day, when we were performing in Ulm, near Stuttgart, my father's sister, Aunt Hannah, appeared in the crowd. She had seen my name on the playbill, and could not believe her eyes. She told me that Uncle Nathan had survived as well and was living in Austria.

I visited Uncle Nathan and his family in Steyr, but after a few months became restless. Making my way on foot to Italy, I met up with two young men in the Alps who were going to Ladispoli, a small town by the sea about 40 kilometres from Rome. Together, we arrived and joined Kibbutz Ma'Pilim.

I was giving music lessons at the kibbutz and decided to apply to the American Joint Committee for funds to purchase a full-sized accordion. I travelled to the AJC office in Rome, where I learned that they were sponsoring one thousand Jewish orphans for entry into Canada. I was told that if I could prove that I was under eighteen, I would be accepted as one of the orphans. Immediately, I went to the central office of the Zionist organization in Rome and, by "correcting" 1928 to 1930 in their records, was able to secure the necessary documentation. At the same time I adopted Jerzyk's birthday, April 28, so that in a sense he would be with me as I began a new life in Canada.

We sailed aboard a Greek ship, the *New Hellas*, docking in Halifax in March of 1948. From there I travelled by train to Toronto, where I was assigned to a social worker who found me a job. In the evenings I performed on a borrowed accordion at fund-raising events. I gave my first performance in Toronto at Holy Blossom Temple in May. A group of us organized the Hebrew Youth Club; our symbol was a tree trunk with a new branch sprouting and the motto "The Few of the Many".

One day I decided to see more of the country and went down to the train station. I had only 5 dollars in my pocket. "How far will 5 dollars take me?" I asked the ticket vendor.

"London, Ontario," came the reply. So I was off to London, where I sought out a local rabbi. He helped me to find a place to stay, and soon I was hired to teach accordion at a music store.

I applied to the armoury of Princess Patricia's Own Fusiliers, a reserve army unit. It was fun learning to drive a tank and doing exercises twice a week, for which I was compensated 2 dollars. I was about to receive my uniform when the sergeant called me in and announced, "You are not a Canadian citizen! How can you be in the army?" That ended my short military career.

In September 1954, I met Sarah Hermine, who became my wife. Herma was about to return to her native Austria. I made her a 5-dollar bet that she would stay in Canada. The next day, Hermine cashed in her ticket. As I write these lines, we have just celebrated out forty-second wedding anniversary. We have raised two musically talented daughters, Deborah and Halina, and we have a beautiful granddaughter, Evelyn Ruth, Deborah's daughter, who just turned ten.

My work life includes eleven years as an electronic techician at Northern Electric and many more selling real estate in Toronto. In addition, I began composing songs again in my forties. One such song, "The Times We Live In" was inspired by the Biafran crisis of 1969. The song was recorded the following year by Salome Bey. I identified with the pictures I had seen of the starving children of Biafra. I was one of them.

The times we live in are not hard for those who
   do not suffer.
Child in pain of hunger will not ask
Why other children elsewhere live, not die.
He does not know, he does not know why he has
   to die.

Can you explain it to him? Can you explain it to
    him?
Oh, can you tell him a handy lie?
Tell him of heaven that's waiting for him,
Where there's no hunger, where there's no pain.
Please do not tell him, please do not tell him,
His only life is spent in vain.*

*Words and music ©1969 by Arthur and Halina Schaller